SAP S/4 HANA Finance Best Practices

Alfonso Colombano
Robert Lee
with special thanks to Chris Bartkoski

Book idea, compilation and authorship by Alfonso Colombano and Robert Lee.

Self-published by Alfonso Colombano and Robert Lee.

Edited by Alfonso Colombano and Robert Lee.

ISBN: **9798713328504**

Printed by Amazon KDP, An Amazon.com Company

www.sapoilgas.com

Disclaimers

All data discussed and used in this book has been referenced and sourced from **publicly** available materials, such as companies' forms 10-K and 20-F, annual reports, internet websites, news articles, company reports, job postings and news releases. Reader should verify accuracy by checking cited references.

SAP is a registered trademark of SAP AG in Germany, SAP SE and several other countries. All other trademarks are the property of their respective owners.

The recommendations, advice, analysis, descriptions, methods and calculations presented in this book are for educational and illustration purposes only. The authors shall not be liable for any income, career or any other loss or any damage that results from the use of any of the material in this book.

Alfonso Colombano, Robert Lee or the book's publishers shall not be liable for any damages whatsoever, and in particular the authors shall not be liable for any special, indirect, consequential, or incidental damages, or damages for lost profits, loss of revenue, or loss of use arising out of or related to this book or the information within, whether such damages arise in contract, negligence, tort, under statute, in equity, at law, or otherwise, even if the authors have been advised of the possibility of such damages.

Table of Contents

About Alfonso Colombano

Alfonso is the author of the bestseller series of books titled *Oil & Gas Company Analysis*, as well *Careers in the Oil & Gas Industry*. Alfonso has worked for three International Oil Companies (IOC's) and one refining company in system, analytical, commercial, financial and IT roles. Alfonso has worked with SAP products for more than 12 years and has experience both as a business *power user* and as a *specialist* in SAP IT projects. Alfonso has worked in the majority of submodules in Finance, as well as has several years of experience in Plant Maintenance, Materials Management, Project Systems and IS-Oil Production Revenue Accounting (PRA).

Alfonso was part of one of the largest greenfield implementations of S/4 Finance in the Oil & Gas Industry. Previously, he was one of the key team members that led the discovery process of implementing SAP S/4 HANA for one of the largest independent downstream companies in the U.S.

Alfonso's expertise encompasses the financial & operational analysis of oil & gas companies, having developed several analytical models for M&A activity and commercial analysis. Alfonso is a well-seasoned public speaker and has been featured at the University of Houston and the *Global Energy Leaders Podcast*. Alfonso enjoys reading books about SAP, the oil & gas industry and playing golf in his free time.

Alfonso can be reached by email at alfonso@sapoilgas.com or by following his LinkedIn page at www.linkedin.com/in/alfonsocolombano

About Robert Lee

A self-proclaimed *uber geek*, Robert began his software development career in academia by co-authoring one of the first omni-data transmission tools before the popularity of HTML. His career diverged to the oil & gas industry when he was employed by IBM and placed at Saudi Aramco in 1996. Shortly after, his continued presence in the petroleum space was solidified by nearly twenty years of software development internally at SAP, including the development team of the SAP PRA project as well as multiple PRA implementations.

In 2007, he co-founded an SAP ISV (independent software vendor) and made available several certified ABAP add-ons for public consumption.

Robert has helped companies improve performance on SAP systems throughout his career. Robert, as an experienced SAP developer, has helped clients around the world improve their S/4 HANA custom and standard performance. These performance improvements have led to clients debottleneck key SAP finance processes and achieve targeted savings.

Robert can be reached by email at robert@sapoilgas.com.

Acknowledgements – Alfonso Colombano

"Gratitude is a mark of a noble soul and a refined character. We like to be around those who are grateful." – Joseph B. Wirthlin

Without the immeasurable aid and support of my wife Indira, parents and siblings who encouraged and assisted me, I would never have completed this lengthy effort.

Secondly to my great friends Robert Lee (co-author) and Chris Bartkoski, who I have learned so much about SAP from a *technical* and *functional* perspective. Robert and Chris' SAP ABAP custom developments have saved companies millions of dollars. Moreover, their kindness and willingness to knowledge share and help out every step of the way is highly admirable. I am very fortunate to have had the chance to work with both of them in several projects. Having started my career in Finance as an SAP power user, I am extremely grateful to both of them for having helped me grow immensely in the SAP technical IT space.

Additionally, I express gratitude to great colleagues, mentors, managers such as, Kathy Epperson, Michael Lewis, Cindy Davis, Antonio Lima, Emeka Oyolu, , Daniel Chiarion, Charlie Gillman, Thompson Franca, Alex Villegas, Sandra Dickey, Arturo Perez, Rick Campbell, JR Irvin, Asavari Oak, Denis Ognev, and many others. I have learned so much from the individuals listed before in many areas, including SAP FI, ABAP, JVA, PRA, Financial Reporting, the oil & gas industry, Agile, and many, many other topics.

Last, but not least, my sincerest thanks to all the great colleagues, supervisors, managers, operations personnel, and mentors that I have had the good fortune to have worked with in the energy and financial industry throughout my career. I have been quite blessed to have been surrounded throughout my career, including at university and at work, with brilliant people who have influenced my views and have helped me tremendously.

Without the help of all of you, I could not have completed this monumental task. Thanks everybody!

Alfonso Colombano
Houston, Texas, USA
March 2021

Acknowledgements – Robert Lee

> *"We must find time to stop and thank the people who make a difference in our lives." – John F. Kennedy*

First and foremost, to my beloved wife Charity. You are my number one fan and it is this knowledge that fuels me and pushes me outside of my comfort zone. With you by my side, I know there is nothing I cannot accomplish. You are the biggest blessing in my life.

Not only is my wife an inspiration to me, her father (may he rest in peace) always believed in me. This one is for you Dad!

To my good friend and co-author, Alfonso Colombano, sincere gratitude for allowing me to take this journey with you. I am both humbled and honored that you invited me onto this project. Truth be told, the term co-author is rather misleading. I would think more than 80% of the book was you. I merely sprinkled it with typos, poor grammar, and the odd piece of potentially useful information. Your knowledge in SAP and the oil and gas industry continues to astound me.

To my partners in crime Rob Schnell, Clint Whitlock, Dale Bruton, Chris Bartkoski, and countless others – thank you for your professionalism, your support, and your friendship. People often say that in order to improve, you need to surround yourself with people better than you. You are all in that company. I am lucky to say that I love my work. It is because of the people I get to work with.

In closing, a major shout-out to all the leads, managers, supervisors in the various companies that I've had the pleasure of working for or interacting with. Thank you for trusting me and recognizing the value that I added to your organization. My career would not be where it is at without your faith in my skills.

Robert Lee
Plano, Texas, USA

March 2021

Preface

"We are stuck with technology when what we really want is just stuff that works." Douglas Adams

Dear reader,

Thank you for choosing this book. This is the fifth book I have published in my career and I am very excited about the contents of this book. An SAP ERP implementation, for all modules, but particularly for Finance, can be quite a complex endeavor. The primary goal of this book is to share *lessons learned, best practices* and *hopefully* help the reader avoid the same mistakes in the future. I hope you enjoy this book and find the chapters in this book applicable to your SAP implementation.

This book will attempt to accomplish the following:

- How is SAP Finance used in many industries? how critical is it for the success of any SAP implementation?
- Provide a set of questions to help readers on their finance implementation.
- Provide *candid, open and applicable* suggestions in several areas of the SAP implementation.
- Emphasize the importance of good ABAP code quality not only in custom programs, but in *reviewing* SAP provided standard programs.
- Setup an environment & processes on how to receive *faster* and more *effective* feedback and *how to use* that input into an SAP implementation.
- Define what *effective* change management is, what change management is not and the *criticality* of change management to an implementation.
- Walk through the reasons *why* performance testing in S/4 is so critical to the success of an implementation.

This book is organized into twelve chapters:

- Chapter I provides an overview of SAP, set of products and modules within an SAP ERP system.

- Chapter II discusses the criticality of all kinds of data in the success of not only an SAP implementation, but even for day-to-day business processes.
- Chapter III provides an overview of the steps required for having an enterprise structure not only to meet the organizational needs of today, but for future requirements of a company.
- Chapter IV presents the different series of events required to setup a successful *end-to-testing* cycle for the implementation.
- Chapter V discusses the *objectives* and different *approaches* to a successful financial data conversion.
- Chapter VI makes the point as to *why* establishing a good *feedback mechanism* is so critical to a successful SAP S/4 Finance implementation.
- Chapter VII makes the case as to *why* having good ABAP *code quality* and outlines the consequences of *not* having good ABAP code.
- Chapter VIII discusses the different types of SAP customizations vs. standard functionality and how to weigh the *pros* and *cons* of customizations.
- Chapter IX introduces change management, particularly as applicable for a *finance* organization
- Chapter X discusses performance testing.
- Chapter XI provides a summary of the topics discussed in the book and finalizes with a decision criteria.

We hope you enjoy this book and learn more about the exciting world of SAP S/4 HANA Finance.

Again, thank you for selecting this book!

Alfonso Colombano
Robert Lee
March 2021

Chapter I - Introduction

"How you gather, manage, and use information will determine whether you win or lose." Bill Gates.

S/4 HANA Finance implementation projects can be some of the most challenging and impactful transformational projects a company can implement. The amount of *research, preparation, planning, execution time* and *cost* of an SAP Finance implementation can be quite substantial. We hope with the recommended practices described in this book your implementation will have a *higher chance* of success. Or at least, we hope with the questions and recommendations in this book, that your implementation will be able to focus on areas for improvements and hopefully avoid large *negative outcomes.*

Audience

Let's discuss a little bit about the *intended* audience of this book. Many readers can benefit from this book, from C-level corporate executives, IT and financial executives, to IT project managers leading SAP implementations to business analysts working for a transformational project. The terms used in this book are a mixture of both standard financial terms, SAP configuration terms as well as more advanced technical topics, including ABAP, code optimization and many others.

Why this book?

There are many SAP Finance books on the market, but very few combine both a *business & financial acumen* and *strong technical* advice. A significant majority of the books in the market are either *step-by-step* SPRO[1] configuration instructions or discuss at a *very high level* the general features and benefits of each new S/4 HANA release. The authors in this case are set to strike a *balance* and provide practical advice with real life examples. To further distinguish this book from others, each chapter will first try to cover the major financial or business aspects, and then finish off with technical highlights and commentary.

The goals of this book are:

- Provide a brief introduction to the functional capabilities of SAP S/4 HANA Finance.

---

[1] SPRO is basically the SAP transaction code for SAP's control panel.

- Provide the readers with a set of *brainstorming* questions so that the reader can better plan their S/4 HANA implementations.
- Avoid common implementation errors encountered in the past.
- Provide commentary or guidelines as to when *it is best* to customize vs. rely on SAP standard functionality.
- Provide background into the *different* feedback mechanisms of an in-house IT department vs. external SAP consultants.
- Provide technical suggestions, particularly in terms of performance optimization, for SAP finance implementations.

What is SAP?

SAP stands for *Systems, Applications & Products*, or in German *Systeme, Anwendungen und Produkte in der Datenverarbeitung*.

Who is SAP SE?

SAP SE[2] is one of the largest business software in the companies in the world, with more than 440,000[3] business customers from all industries and sectors in the world economy. SAP, as of fiscal year 2019[4], had revenues of more than €27 billion, IFRS[5] earnings of €3.4 billion and more than €60 billion in assets.

What is an ERP?

ERP stands for Enterprise Resource Planning. An ERP is a suite or series of software applications that provides customers with business process software for different applications. An ERP is typically best suited for medium and large enterprises looking to having a central system whereby a multitude of business processes can be performed in a single application. An ERP can have multiple uses, from a purely financials only SAP implementation to most commonly core business processes such as Order to Cash (OTC), Customer relations management (CRM), Procure to Pay (PTP), Plant Maintenance (PM), Materials Management (MM), Project Systems (PS), Financial Accounting (FI), Controlling (CO) and many more. The key advantage of an ERP system is the *centralization of processes* which allows large and medium companies achieve *economies of scale*. After the Sarbanes Oxley

---

[2] SE stands for *Societas Europea* is a public company registered in accordance with corporate law in the European Union. A couple of years ago, SAP was incorporated according to the laws of Germany, therefore, it carried the designation *Aktien-Gesselchaft* or AG

[3] SAP Fourth-Quarter and Full-Year 2019 Preliminary Results Release, page 11

[4] IBID, pages 25 & 30

[5] International Financial Reporting Standards, or IFRS, is the most widely used accounting standards around the world. The closest competitor, primarily due to United States' large capital is U.S. GAAP.

Act of 2002, many companies had to restructure internally their organizations and provide a more *controlled* environment to certify that financial reporting is in compliance with the company's internal control standards. This certification, which has to be done at the CEO, CFO and Controller level on the SEC[6] filings, incentivizes companies to get ERP software since they can provide a better control framework and avoid segregation of duties and potential issues of fraud or misrepresentation of the financial statements.

Why is SAP so ubiquitous among large companies?

There are many reasons why SAP is quite ubiquitous among large and increasingly in medium-sized businesses. SAP ERP and now S/4 HANA provide companies with a way of integrating disparate business processes, from logistics, procurement, sales, materials resource planning, plant maintenance, scheduling, projects and finance into a single solution. From a financial perspective, SAP, particularly for large companies, has a very *structured* and *scalable* set of user roles and access that allows companies to comply against statutory requirements for internal controls to produce *reliable* and *accurate* financial reporting. Among some of the benefits SAP provides to customers:

- Integration of business processes, the ability for basically any *business event* or *transaction* in SAP to automatically create all sorts of financial records in *real time*. Ever since R/3 and prior versions of SAP, the ability to have the financial statements updated in real time while the transaction is posted has been a key selling point of SAP. With S/4 HANA the analytics capabilities of SAP Finance have taken a great leap forward and for many cases it is no longer necessary to have a separate *financial consolidation system*[7] from the transactional processing system.

- Standardization of processes in a company. By having a unified single system where most, if not all, business processes are contained in the same application, allows users to benefit from a unified user interface, user experience and minimize the number of system reconciliations between different systems.

---

[6] United States Securities & Exchange Commission, is the agency in charge of all financial regulation dealing with the capital markets. In the context of this SAP Finance implementations, the SEC has a direct impact on the required financial disclosures and thus impacts an ERP system like SAP indirectly.
[7] Example of financial consolidation systems include Hyperion Financial Management (owned by Oracle) or SAP Business Consolidation System (BCS)

- Provides a controlled environment, where *segregation of duties* can be enforced to a large extent[8]. This is particularly a *non-negotiable* requirement in an *increasingly* regulated financial and securities market[9].

History of SAP ERP

SAP started their software development with RM/1 in the 1970's, then R/2 in the 1980's and early 1990s. In 1992, R/3 was released, which incorporated many substantial improvements over R/2. R/3 was the first version of SAP ERP that moved away from mainframe processing which was used with R/2.

ECC 6.0 is the *last major stable* version of SAP's traditional ERP R/3 product, with several so-called *Enhancements Packs* which provide additional functionality, security patches and bug fixes. The latest stable release as of the time of this writing is Enhancement Pack 8 for ECC 6.0

On the other hand, NetWeaver is the technical foundation for many of SAP products, including SAP ERP and S/4 HANA. As of the time of writing of this book, the latest available version of NetWeaver is NW AS ABAP 7.52.

Evolution of SAP HANA

Although HANA Database has been available since the early 2010's, S/4 HANA was officially launched in 2015. As of the time of publication, SAP S/4 HANA has more than 13,000 licensed customers[10] that have implemented a version of S/A HANA.

S/4 HANA can be hosted *on-premise[11]*, in the cloud, or a hybrid combination of the two.

S/4 HANA Finance has been evolving through different version releases. SAP usually names versions of S/4 HANA based on the *year* and *month* the changes were released. So, for example version *1503* was released in 2015 in the month of March, version *1909* in 2019 in the month of September and so forth. Hana Database versions are a little bit simpler and they started with

---

[8] Depends heavily on the security design of an implementation, but SAP has excellent tools such as *Governance, Risk and Compliance* or GRC that provides pre-built checks for analyzing roles which could cause Segregation of Duties (SOD) conflicts (i.e. a role having creation of purchase orders, goods receipt or invoice approval posting combined).

[9] ERP software has experienced substantial growth, in part due to the passage of laws such as Sabarnes & Oxley Act (SOX) of 2002, which require the CEO, CFO and Controller of a company to attest to the effectiveness of the company's internal controls on filings with the SEC. Thus having an ERP with robust SOD functionality is key.

[10] SAP Fourth-Quarter and Full-Year 2019 Preliminary Results Release, page 5

[11] On-premise means that the software runs on hardware operated by the customer.

HDB version 1.0 and different incremental *Support Pack Stacks* or SPS. These SPS are released every couple of years with the latest stable release being HDB 2.0 SPS 04.

Advantages of S/4 HANA Finance

S/4 HANA Finance, *previously marketed as SAP Simple Finance[12]*, provides many improvements, as well as many challenges, over prior versions of SAP ERP. One of the key philosophical concepts of S/4 Finance is the *simplification* of the data model of financial processes, including the consolidation of previously isolated financial tables into a single Universal Journal[13]. This feature was not technically possible before due to limitations in database technology. Now with *in-memory* database technology, such as HANA, millions of data records can be summarized on the *fly* in a couple of seconds, instead of the hours or even days it could take before. This key feature provides many benefits but also as well presents several challenges, which will be discussed later in the book.

Among the key simplifications in S/4 HANA Finance:

- Combines separate financial tables which before were separate, including, totals tables, line items tables and index tables. These tables have now, or in the future become *one single* table, the so-called *Universal Journal* or in technical speak ACDOCA table. Tables such as BKPF, BSEG, COEP, COBK and many others, which in ECC were in separate tables, their data has now become part of the Universal Journal (ACDOCA) table.

- By using an in-memory database, S/4 HANA can provide enhanced analytical tools and simplify the retrieval of data for reporting and analysis purposes. Many custom reports can be built from a *single data source*, simplifying data storage as well as reducing the need to have *redundant* or *duplicative* data, with the associated data reconciliation required to be in sync. Additionally, the use of an in-memory database can improve the amount of time spent in developing new custom programs since data can be queried from a single source of data. In other words, the process discovery for custom developments is reduced by relying on a single source of financial data.

---

[12] https://www.sap.com/products/s4hana-finance-erp.html
[13] The Universal Journal technical name is ACDOCA table.

- SAP provides the concept of "model companies" for faster prototyping, which allow to demo the capabilities as well as assist with the actual implementation of the system. The model company concept allows new companies implementing SAP to transition and deploy S/4 HANA faster than before. These model companies come pre-configured with key steps in the SPRO[14] already completed for those companies. Model companies also include key master data like a pre-configured chart of accounts, cost centers, profit centers and many more master data setups so that new companies can transition to S/4 HANA faster than before. Having all these *pre-requisite steps* already configured in the systems allows a company to basically "model" their implementation on the most *widely used* SAP Finance functionality and save a significant amount of time and dollars in process discovery. In addition, by basing your configuration on a model company many costly configuration mistakes can be avoided.

Business Processes within S/4 HANA Finance

S/4 HANA Finance encompasses a variety of business processes for modern Finance and Accounting organizations for multiple industries. Among the areas that S/4 HANA Finance can help with are[15]:

- Cost management and profitability
- Subscription billing
- Accounting and financial close
- Revenue accounting and reporting
- Treasury management
- Financial operations
- Enterprise risk and compliance

Modules in SAP S/4 HANA Finance

S/4 Finance comes with a series of modules, some fully optimized for HANA, with others still evolving from a data model perspective from the prior ECC 6 world.

---

[14] SPRO can be thought of SAP's "Control Panel" where many of the functionalities can be configured in that area. SPRO contains most if not all the configuration transaction codes used typically by the IT organization.

[15] https://www.sap.com/products/s4hana-erp/features/finance.html

FI

Finance or simply, FI, encompasses multiple functionality such as:

- Accounts Receivable (AR), integrated with several modules that create AR such as Sales & Distribution, Project systems, JVA and many more. AR is used by departments such as receivables management, customer service, sales, credit and many others. This module can provide these users a real-time view of customer balances, payments, new sales, uncollected amounts and other functionality.

- General Ledger (GL), similar to ECC 6.0, provides a full set of functionalities of *core financial accounting* processes such as posting financial entries, reversing entries, clearing open items, maintaining a GL account master data, reporting account balances and much more. The general ledger is the *ultimate repository* of all financial transactions that occur in an enterprise system. The GL submodule provides the basis for financial reporting and financial consolidation, particularly for those users in groups such as financial accounting, consolidations, tax compliance and reporting and others. The GL module can provide a full balance sheet and income statement by a variety of criteria such as company code or business area. The general ledger basis of reporting in S/4 is now table ACDOCA, with *more than 400* standard fields, provides a very flexible reporting not just for financial transactions but also for operational and financial KPI reporting.

- Accounts Payable (AP), with integration with materials management, allows users to *review, process* and *approve* invoices, make vendor payments and reconcile vendor balances. Additionally, accounts payable provides key integration into a variety of sales and use tax and value-added tax applications. Applications such as TaxWare[16] facilitate the *recording, payment* and *compliance* of these geographically-determined taxes.

- Banking (BK), with integration into banking interfaces, provides customers with the ability to make and receive payments from different associated banks, reconcile bank account, issue payments, apply cash receipts and many other critical features. Banking

---

[16] Taxware is vendor that provides U.S. sales and use tax solutions for applications like SAP. Taxware uses as variety of fields in SAP to determine *geographically* where the sale or purchase has taken place so that the company can successfully comply with the very complex indirect tax regulations in the U.S. and other countries.

functionality is tightly integrated with AR, AP, HR and other modules in SAP so that a full end-to-end view of the impacts of baking transactions are processed in real-time in SAP. Banking is one of the areas where more and more progress has been made in converting functionality into Fiori[17] from the traditional SAP GUI.

CO

The CO or Controlling module in Finance is responsible primarily for *managerial accounting type* functionality and includes the following:

- Cost element accounting, a cost element provides a way to *allocate*[18] and *settle*[19] costs from one cost object to the other. In S/4, the creation of cost elements has been simplified by having these cost elements created in the same transaction code as regular GL accounts. In other words, there are no separate tables that store cost elements vs. GL accounts as it was before in ECC 6.0.

- Cost center accounting, now in S/4 HANA Finance integrated in ACDOCA, allows a corporation to *record* and *conduct* cost analysis at the *lowest level possible*. Cost center accounting allows a corporation to be able to track costs at each individual cost center as well as to perform allocation and settlement of costs from one cost center to the other. Cost center accounting functionality in S/4 is simplified by having the results of CO activity stored directly in ACDOCA, while before it relied on different tables such as COEP, COBK, and many others. This change in S/4 simplifies the data model extensively so that allocations and settlements can be traced forward and back *directly* in the universal journal and not have to reconcile with different tables as before. In S/4 HANA, by design, there is no longer a FI-CO reconciliation process.

- Internal Orders, similar to cost center accounting is now also fully integrated into ACDOCA. Internal orders, unlike cost centers, are *temporary* cost objects[20], so they must always *settle* or *allocate* on a

---

[17] Fiori will be discussed further in the book, but basically is a new SAP interface that allows to "run" SAP in multiple devices include desktop, mobile phones and tables. Fiori's goal is to make the SAP user interface significantly more user friendly than before with the SAP GUI.

[18] Allocations are a way of sharing costs from one place to the other. An example is $100 cost that should be borne by two cost centers. The CO module can allocate or share this cost into two $50 transactions for each cost centers. Allocations can get quite complex and are beyond the scope of this book.

[19] Settlements are used widely in the SAP world. A key example of this is for assets-under-construction, whereby costs are collected and then settled periodically to a fixed assets AUC.

[20] A cost object, as the name implies, is an object that holds costs. Cost centers, internal orders, work orders and WBS elements are all examples of cost objects.

periodic basis to a *permanent* cost object. Internal orders can be a very powerful functionality that allow a company to setup ad-hoc cost responsibility capabilities. Say for example a department wanted to track a special training that occurs once a year, they could setup an internal order that collects all costs associated with that training. Then the costs of this training internal order would still settle or move back to the department cost center but based on the *settlement*[21] or *distribution*[22]. Being that internal order accounting is now fully embedded in the main financial table, it is now easier than ever to see the flow of costs in a single table, instead of the multiple tables before.

- Profit Center Accounting, now in S/4 HANA Finance integrated in ACDOCA. Profit center accounting, coupled with *document splitting*[23] functionality, allows a company to have a *fully balanced* set of books by profit center. This fully balanced set of books provides, for example, the ability to calculate *return on inventory*, *return on capital employed* and many other financial metrics. Profit Center Accounting can provide many financial insights in an organization and allow to have financial statements lower than the company code. Keep in mind that having a robust profit center structure (covered in a further chapter) is *highly critical* to a successful SAP S/4 HANA Finance implementation.

PS

Although typically thought of part of the Logistics area and not Finance, Project Systems is tightly integrated into finance. Project systems gives a customer the ability to create work breakdown structures (WBS) elements for project *planning*, *budgeting* and *recording* of actual costs. These WBS elements can be created as lower down in detail or at a higher level and allow for planning the different project phases or element. Once actual costs are booked to these WBS elements, they can then be settled into either assets under construction (AUC) for capital projects or to a cost center for expense projects. PS functionality has continued to evolve in S/4 HANA, similar to CO module, in the fact that postings are integrated into the universal journal,

---

[21] A settlement is a flow of costs that go from a cost object to another, typically summarizing the multiple costs collected into a single or a handful of cost elements.
[22] A distribution, unlike a settlement, is basically *in and out* in the sense that the very same cost elements used to record the transaction in the cost object are then used to move costs to the other cost object.
[23] Document Splitting is an SAP functionality that basically *balances* out a financial posting in an FI document by pre-selected characteristics beyond company code (i.e. profit center, business area, etc…)

simplifying as well the data model. This change also simplifies the settlement process, no longer having to rely on tables like COEP.

FA

Fixed Assets, is a critical component of SAP Finance. Fixed assets module provides a customer the ability to *create, track* and *retire* asset records all throughout the asset lifecycle, from original asset under construction settlement, to running depreciation and much more. There are many changes in S/4 Finance, some which may cause significant performance issues as SAP continues to transition to a full universal journal integration. Fixed assets will continue to evolve in future S/4 HANA versions as SAP migrates more and more functionality (for example non-financial depreciation area postings) into the Universal Journal.

CO-PA

Although typically thought as a module within the controlling module, CO-PA is so complex and powerful and tightly integrated with SD and MM modules that it is typically cataloged as its own individual module. There are two types of CO-PA, *account-based* and *cost-based*. Account-based CO-PA is now fully integrated into the Universal Journal, although the most powerful version, CO-PA cost-based, will likely continue to be a separate *ledger* in future S/4 versions. CO-PA allows a customer to be able to calculate profitability at very low levels, including sales orders, customer level and much more. CO-PA is truly an excellent analytical & reporting tool which allows for economic analysis and for customers to provide better decisions on pricing, gross margin and much more.

Oil & Gas Industry Specific Modules

SAP has had a presence in the oil & gas industry since the 1990's, improving its software offering over the years. Some of the largest SAP enterprise customers are oil & gas companies, with the majority of integrated oil & gas companies running SAP since the early 1990's.

Production Revenue Accounting (PRA)

This module is built specifically to account for oil & gas revenues for companies with U.S. operations. Since royalty ownership and state regulations can be quite complex, SAP acquired the former Premas software from PriceWaterhouse in the late 1990's and has continued to add more functionality. PRA is a specialty module on its own, with only companies with U.S. exploration & production operations (upstream) using this module. To become a true expert in PRA takes several years of practice and throughout this book we will not cover as much as of PRA areas since the audience is intended to be *general finance application*.

Production Sharing Agreement

Much smaller than U.S. PRA, Production Sharing Agreement module attempts to provide functionality for international operations of oil & gas companies. One of the challenges with this module is that every country can be quite different and require significant customizations. SAP has created this module particularly tailored to large international oil & gas companies like Chevron, Shell and many others.

Joint Venture Accounting

Joint venture accounting was one of the first specifically targeted modules for the oil & gas industry in the 1990's. Joint venture is used primarily by upstream oil & gas companies looking for a solution to provide accounting functionality for joint interest or joint ventures. The vast majority of operations in the oil & gas industry, primarily due to risk-sharing considerations, are done through joint ventures. JVA can be quite complex and it is one of the modules that it is still not fully enabled in the universal journal and requires its own *special ledger*. Future versions of JVA are expected to merge *over time* to a new data model in the universal journal[24].

Technical Point of View

People familiar with SAP will no doubt know that SAP products change names throughout their lifecycle for various reasons (technical, marketing, etc.) To avoid confusion, here are some explanations of nomenclature used by SAP from a technical point of view.

HANA

SAP HANA Database was leading the charge in the last decade. One can say that it may even have origins in *LiveCache* as well as other legacy SAP products. As memory prices decrease, the notion of computing using memory instead of hard drives was more plausible. Memory density also helped in this endeavor. HANA DB was one of the first *in memory column store* databases in the market. With HANA DB 1.0, SAP customers running ERP 6.0 could actually migrate and operate their system what is commonly known as Business Suite on HANA (Business Suite was the collective name

---

[24] https://blogs.sap.com/2019/09/23/sap-s4hana-1909-innovation-highlights-of-the-intelligent-suite/

given to ECC, SRM, CRM, HCM, etc.) For those following closely, it is basically running R/3 on HANA DB.

S/4 HANA

To capitalize on the major performance advantages of HANA DB, SAP decided to revamp major parts of its legacy R/3 ERP software starting with the most used component – FI/CO (Finance/Controlling). The generally accepted database software design for several decades beforehand was to de-normalize the data model. Denormalizing basically means to refactor the data in such a way that only the essential information is stored in one database table thus saving space and increasing querying speed. Multiple tables are used to store one real world transaction to avoid data duplication. This technique however does NOT take advantage of HANA. Because HANA stores the majority of its tables in column store (with compression), denormalization no longer makes sense. Having large (wide) database tables is preferred by HANA. So, SAP "simplified" the FI/CO modules by migrating a large portion of the transactional database tables into one unified "super table" (ACDOCA). This simplification is the drive behind the new marketing name S/4 HANA. HANA is so efficient at *reading* large amounts of data from single tables that near real time analysis of data is possible. This is one of the true innovations behind S/4 HANA. Just the database itself is *not* sufficient. The revamp of the data model is a *must* to take full advantage.

S/4 HANA Finance

Since S/4 HANA is really the next version of Business Suite – it actually includes the original ERP modules, FI, CO, SD, MM, PM, SM, etc. The simplified version of FI (since not all ERP modules have made the transformation or simplification) was originally marketed as Simple Finance but now called S/4 HANA Finance. For customers already using Business Suite, SAP provides a roadmap to migrate using the Migration Cockpit. There are prescribed and tested ways to minimize downtime and problems during cutover. With each update of S/4 HANA, more modules and processes are being revamped and simplified. SAP's website provides an excellent features roadmap showing you what is in the near future[25].

NetWeaver

The unsung hero, the backend servers which actually performs all the business functions, has changed its name many times. What was originally

---

[25] https://go.support.sap.com/roadmapviewer. For customers without an S-ID, they can access without having to login.

known as the application server, became the web application server, evolved into split servers (ABAP and Java), and eventually back together again as a unified server which runs in an S/4 landscape. Names aside, in the new S/4 landscape, different servers run in tandem to provide the technical backbone. In a basic S/4 technical landscape, the HANA database would generally run on its own server (for hardware, software, and performance reasons). Classic application servers continue to serve as they have in R/3. In addition, various servers like Adobe Services or Fiori Frontend can also be part of the seamless ecosystem.

Technical Topology

Traditionally, SAP R/3 systems were *on premise* behemoths requiring dedicated data centers. With everything shifting to the cloud, S/4 HANA has that covered. S/4 HANA can be on-premise like any other R/3 system. Understand the term *on-premise* here is not *geography specific*. One can have an S/4 HANA installation hosted by a cloud vendor (e.g. Amazon Web Services). The on-premise designation has more to do with the installation and maintenance of the software itself. In the case of AWS, the "hardware" is of course provided by and maintained by Amazon. But the customer is allowed to do anything with the software as they please (within the bounds of the licensing agreement of course). Contrast that to a true S/4 HANA Cloud Edition implementation whereby SAP actually is hosting S/4 HANA and offering it up as a SaaS (Software as a Service) and the customer merely pays for user on a periodic basis. The maintenance of the software is included in the rental. To the end user, all of the above topologies yield the same end result. Only difference may be speed (since cloud deployed scenarios depend heavily on a robust WAN connection). Each variation offers different pros and cons and should be studied diligently before deciding.

Fiori

What is Fiori exactly? Thru acquisition of a third-party company, SAP shed its old look and feel and adopted a brand new visually stimulating user interface. The classic SAP transactional screens still exist and continue to perform a lot of major lifting within the system. Fiori is a web front end along with a set of common themed templates which provide a total user experience[26]. More than just a pretty screen, Fiori allowed SAP to create a *consistent* and *easy* to use portal into S/4 HANA. Using the provided Fiori Launchpad, users are able to bypass the legacy SAP menu and gain access to

---

[26] For additional information on the different versions of Fiori, please visit
https://experience.sap.com/news/sap-fiori-how-it-started-and-where-its-going/

the new Fiori applications as well as traditional SAP transactions. More Fiori applications are being provided with each new S/4 HANA release. Regardless of what a new Fiori application may do, it will always follow the same core principles:

- Role Based: Users are not cluttered with items they are not interested in or have no access to like the old SAP menu. They only see what *they need* to perform *their job*.
- Delightful: One's job should not be a burden. The software *should not* get in the way of the user, but instead *enhance* their work experience.
- Coherent: Common sets of controls, themes, patterns, layouts allow for ease in adoption.
- Simple: Straight and to the point, simplified screens allow for increase in job efficiency.
- Adaptive: Regardless of the device used (PC, tablet, mobile phone), the user experience should be *consistent*.

Note that Fiori was already available *prior* to S/4 HANA. It was able to run on a separate server providing, at that time, a smaller set of Fiori applications to Business Suite on HANA. With S/4 HANA, Fiori is *fully integrated* but for performance reasons can be *decoupled* and utilize a dedicated cluster of frontend servers – similar to performance techniques used for webservers.

Chapter II – Data, Data, Data

"One of the unseen inhibitors to ERP utilization is that ERP software assumes that there are no departmental or process conflicts existing with the customer. All are aligned and in harmony with each other." Brett Beaubouef

Data as an asset

The mantra of *"data as an asset"* is widely repeated in all types of publications and media in general. In the context of an ERP implementation, all types of data, both *master data* and *transactional data* are highly critical. One of the most important steps is to conceptually evaluate how the different flows of data will be *created, processed, transformed* or *posted* throughout the system.

Different types of data

An ERP system consists of different types of data, primarily master data and transactional data.

Both master data and transactional data are very valuable for a company not only to be able to perform daily activities, but also to truly utilize its ERP system as a valuable analysis tool and generate business *insights* from the vast amounts of data being generated. Looking back at prior implementations, bad data has been a significant culprit of *less than ideal* returns on SAP implementations[27].

Master Data

Master data can be defined as the set of data which is *commonly used* across the entire organization and *all business processes*[28]. For example, a General Ledger account will not only be used by financial processes, but across other processes such as procure to pay, order to cash, maintenance operations and many other. The same with a cost center.

Transactional Data

Transactional data, as the name implies, is the *structured data* generated or created arising from transactions or business events. In finance, examples of transactional data include financial documents posted or invoices posted.

---

[27] https://www.computerweekly.com/news/252435884/Chances-of-success-with-SAP-are-only-50-50
[28] https://www.technosap.com/sap-overview/sap-master-data/

Definitions of master data

Having a widely shared and *well-understood* master data definitions across the organization is very important. For example, does the definition of what constitutes a cost center *similar* across different departments or business units, or is it all over the place? Are GL accounts used *consistently* across the different businesses or departments or does each department create them as they go? Knowing *ahead* of the implementation what the different groups in your company *interpret* or *use* a cost center for is highly beneficial. Many times, during implementation projects, stark conceptual differences would arise late into the project, potentially impacting the ultimate success of the SAP Finance implementation.

Data validation

Having a good approach for data validation is quite important in an ERP system. For example, when creating a cost center in most SAP systems, the system has a built-in validation to derive the *tax jurisdiction code* from the cost center's address. This is an example of a validation *before* the data is created or posted.

Some other forms of data validation can occur as a transaction is being posted. For example, a basic validation built-in to SAP FI is that *every document* must be *fully balanced* (i.e. debits equal credits), which takes place as the document is about to be posted.

Lastly, we would have one of the most expensive method, which is an *after-the-fact* validation. This would encompass a vast majority of accounting processes, including account reconciliations, variance analysis and many others. The farther along from the master or transactional data the validation would be, the *more expensive* it would become to fix it in the initial transaction.

As you implement your SAP solution, think about what sorts of validations or checks can be created to help mitigate *data quality* risks. Many implementations have failed due to having poor quality data, both master and transactional data. A good example is to design FI validations and substitutions[29] were applicable in order to mitigate the risks of having incorrect transactional data. For master data, enabling robust definitions of

---

[29] Validations (t-code GGB0) and Substitutions (t-code GGB1) are standard functionality in SAP which allow customers to validate or substitute key fields in a variety of business processes. Validations and substitutions can use a constant value, but more than likely would require a user-exit. A user exit is a customization point whereby an SAP customer can add their own ABAP code at *predefined exit points* without impacting the core functionality in SAP.

every master data fields and centralizing the creation of this data is quite important.

Criticality of full end-to-end flow of data

Throughout many projects, one of the causes seen time and time again for not having detected significant bugs earlier in testing, involved not having comprehensive *data scenarios*. It is quite important to have these scenarios built-out in *advance* with the most critical data fields to be tested. Moreover, in most ERPs, and particularly with SAP, it is quite complex to be able to correct large errors in transactional data *after* data has already been created or posted.

Say a critical field like trading partner[30] is missing from 2 months of financial postings originating in a *feeder module*, how would the organization be able to re-post financial transactions to accounting periods that are already closed? How would the organization be able to know, re-process and know the counter-party company code to each relevant transaction that was posted?

Moreover, for the person or group processing these transactions, the trading partner field in this case would not be a critical field that they would get an *immediate feedback* for posting incorrectly. For example, whether the actual trading partner was right or not, would not *prevent* a user from continuing the posting (if the field is required and it is populated, the transaction will post). This is why many organizations implement validations not just to ensure that a field is *populated*, but that a *valid combination* is selected.

Several recommendations:

- Start with the *last report* or *process* in the chain of data flow and handovers. From a financial perspective, you would typically find these reports in areas such as financial or external reporting, tax areas (whether compliance or financial accounting) or in other internal reporting groups. Think about which processes in the Account to Report groups of processes are *farther* away from a transaction and work backwards to the originating transaction. These processes have a lot of dependencies and if not addressed at the *beginning* would typically be missed.

---

[30] Trading Partner in SAP is a field that denotes the *counterpart* company code to a transaction. Say a sale between one company code and the other would have a trading partner typically on the *sale side* although sometimes could be seen on both (sales and purchases).

- Start documenting and creating *awareness* of which data fields are *critical* for these reports. By going through these steps, it would help identify process *dependencies* and help your team understand the data dependencies between different groups and business processes.
- Start listing out which typical elements in the financial space would be important for standard financial reporting. Examples of these elements in Finance include trading partner, volumetric data, ownership percentages for gross/net calculations, vendor characterization, tax jurisdiction code and many more.
- Take a couple of these critical fields and start mapping them *backwards* from a data flow perspective and be sure to understand *how* the data is *handed over* and possibly *transformed*. Is the ultimate result captured at the time of transaction or is it assigned via an *after-the-fact* process? How reliable is this process? What are the master data dependencies necessary for this field to be populated *during* the creation of a transactions? What happens if this field is wrong, how would the different groups know?

Organizational Culture and impacts to Data

Organizational culture around data can definitely impact your SAP Finance implementation. Here are some sample questions to thing about organizational culture:

- One of the biggest challenges to have an organizational culture that values data is the existence of *department* or *group* siloes. For a group or department, a data field may seem as *irrelevant* or at most a *nuisance* piece of data to be *coped with*, while for another group that *same field* would be the most critical piece of information in the entire transaction. To what extent you have siloes in your organization will impact the value *all data* will have.
- Is data increasingly seen as IT's responsibility or does the ownership and stewardship of the data clearly reside with the most impacted department or group?
- How SAP *literate* are key transformational executives in the company? Do they have a good comprehension of the technical implications of SAP processes and the complexity of reversing *bad quality data* in the system?
- Do you have a strong group of business analysts, with a good finance background, which are fluent in SAP and have an appreciation for data? It is quite important to have the *right* combination of skillsets,

with individuals leading the transformation having *both* business acumen and a strong technical background.

- Do the analysts in your team have different sets of background in the company? Do all of them come from the same department or have they seen *both sides* of the discussion in a sense? For example, for somebody who has worked in transactional accounting all their life it would be difficult for them to readily empathize with the *data challenges* of say financial reporting or tax compliance. For a staff member that has worked all their careers in financial reporting, they may not appreciate the transactional complexity that each SAP posting requires and may brush those concerns as not relevant. It is good to have a team with a diverse set of career experiences as to avoid *group think*.

Interfaces

As your implementation continues, one of the most impactful reviews or design process that should be completed is around *interfaces*, both *inbound* and *outbound* to your SAP system. Following are a set of questions to think about interfaces:

- How is the data *exchanged* between SAP and the other interfaces? Is it through flat files, APIs[31] or other?
- Does additional processing need to take place or does it depend on a *parallel hierarchy*? For example, say tax jurisdiction code resides in the cost center, is that piece of data sent from the interface or is it derived from the cost center in SAP? What happens if that field is out of sync between the two systems, which one prevails?
- What would happen if SAP were to receive or send incorrect data? Are there control mechanisms or a way to validate in the other system? What are the reports in SAP that would make this incorrect data stand out? If none are available, it would be a good idea to start thinking about building those reports now as to avoid a data quality issue from becoming larger and larger *post SAP go-live*.
- What type of errors would occur? Would they be readily identified due to the transaction not processing (i.e. early feedback mechanism) or would the error be identified in a very distant process (for example through the 1099 process in the U.S. when accounts payable would realize that vendor payments were incorrect?) Focus on those errors

---

[31] Application Programming Interfaces

most likely to occur down the data chain than those that would stop the process completely. The ones that would stop the process completely would probably be identified in unit testing or acceptance testing, while those errors that result in data issues may not be identified months or years after the initial go-live.

- Do the other teams have the *same understanding* of what each data field is supposed to represent or have they made assumptions? Many times, it is quite relevant to go field-by-field and go through the definition and examples for each one to minimize miscommunication between say your SAP team and the other IT team building out an interface.

Data in testing as a risk reduction tool

Investing *early on* in having a good, extensive and representative sample set of both master and transactional data would allow your SAP implementation to go significantly smoother during the different rounds of testing. In many prior SAP implementations before, data errors are found during *go-live*, a few months or even one year later after go-live, significantly increasing the costs of fixing that data and potentially creating an unsolvable issue.

Capturing or creating these different sets of data scenarios can be many times a challenge since the system is not live yet. It is generally advised to carve out a significant amount of time out of your project to *plan* and *create* these different data scenarios as they would help reduce data quality risk in your implementation.

Below are some example steps or guidance you can use for your SAP Finance implementation:

- Starting out with the critical reports *further removed* from a transaction, can the experts in that group let you know what are the needed fields to have a successful report? For example, start with the income tax compliance group in your company, can they provide which fields are needed for a particular tax return?
- For example, it is fairly easy for SAP to provide total *sales*, but about what some of the *additional* criteria needed for tax purposes, such as *location* of where sales occurred? What about having to differentiate from *intra* and *inter* company sales? What about volumetric or other non-currency data needed?
- What other transactional data elements are derived from existing master data? How is that master data generated in the system?

- Beware of unit conversions. Where in the transaction does unit conversion occur? What would happen if the unit conversion factors are incorrect? Generally, the *further down* the process unit conversion is done from the actual transaction being captured, the more likely it is the possibility of changing unit conversions. If a transaction was captured originally with the incorrect unit of measure, then that transaction would have to be reversed out and re-posted again.

- If migrating from a prior non-SAP system, it is imperative to have a cross reference or table of old fields needed for reporting and the new fields in SAP. That way, potential testing data can be designed based on the old system and incorporating the different requirements for a successful financial posting in SAP.

Technical Point of View

How can one increase data quality? What can be done if bad data sneaks into the system and is allowed to propagate? While not perfect, SAP does provide some technical tools to ease the burden of tracking this data (good or bad). These tools have long been available and can be used to provide a partial audit trail.

Table Change Logs

Every SAP transparent database table can have table changes enabled. This can be set in the data dictionary[32]. All changes made to this table are logged regardless and can be reviewed at a later time (e.g. during an audit). It tracks *before* and *after* values as well as *who* changed the data and *when*. However, this technique is mainly used for configuration changes. Unlike repository objects, there is no version control for table entries. So, this tracking of table entry changes was introduced to combat that issue. It has its drawbacks. It is only recommended for use to capture configuration data changes. The table which captures this delta can grow very large very quickly. Moreover, this feature has to be enabled in a productive environment/client. In general, it is *only* used in a development environment since the idea is that configuration never changes in a productive environment without a change from the development system (some exceptions do exist).

Change Documents

So, what about master data changes? How can those be tracked? SAP provided what is known as change documents. Similar to the table change log, change documents is a programmatic solution to track data which has

---

[32] SAP t-code SE11

been changed. The emphasis here is the word "programmatic". While table change logs can be enabled with a flip of a setting in the data dictionary, change documents involve ABAP development. A change document object has to be created AND used by a program / transaction. Just the mere existence of the change document object does not mean anything will be tracked. It just defines what *circumstances* and what *type* of data will be recorded if invoked. The calling program has to create the change document when it detects a change it wants to capture. If all of the above criteria are met, then a change document will be created and can be reviewed or audited in the future. These change documents live in sets of generic SAP database tables and also grow very quickly if not kept in check. So, practice a bit of restrain and only log or capture what is truly *necessary*. While technically possible to use change documents for non-master data, given the nature of how it works, it is *not recommended* for transactional data changes.

Quality versus Quantity

One can never stress enough the importance of data quality. But what about quantity? Even with advancements of HANA in column compression techniques, the database will grow quicker than one would think. Imagine the scenario outlined earlier where the incorrect trading partner was used and a month's worth of financial postings were made before discovering the issue. Supposed that you know what the correct trading partner should be, the proper way of correcting this snag would be to *reverse all the previously made* incorrect financial entries and then rebook them using the correct value. Just this one simple event would have at a minimum *tripled* the number of financial entries made in the system. Data compression of a column is most effective for *non-numeric* data. Numeric data tends to have too large of a range to make compression efficient. So, a large portion of the tripled data will not be compressed. As one can see, size of the database only seems to get larger with time. While HANA is an evolutionary piece of technology, it comes with an appropriate price. Unlike traditional relationship databases, HANA is tied to the hardware (i.e. memory size of the HANA appliance) and increasing the size of HANA is not trivial in comparison.

Thresholds

The current release of the HANA database has a limit of roughly 2 billion rows per table. This is inherent to the hashing identifiers it employs to tag records. HANA administrators have health check reports which notifies them when certain tables are getting close to this threshold. So, what can be done when a table gets close or reaches 2 billion? Partition! Just like

RDBMS[33] of yesteryears, the DBA[34] can partition a table or split the data into multiple segments. Each table's partition scheme can be unique to its usage or access. SAP continues to release *smarter* and more *flexible* ways to partition large tables to provide the customer the flexibility to fit their unique needs. The design of how to partition a table is the sole responsibility of the customer. SAP provides no guidance on this topic except the *pros* and *cons* of each partitioning scheme. Careful analysis is needed to understand usage patterns *before* selecting a portioning scheme.

Archiving to the Rescue

Instead of upgrading to larger HANA appliances, what else could one do to combat data growth? SAP Archiving has been used for decades. Simply put, it allows the removal of "business complete" data from the database thus reducing the size. And what exactly is considered business complete? Any data which is not acted upon anymore. Data which will NOT change and in general be used for as an audit trail. The process of archiving is a technical one. Technical archive objects are involved and the "purged" data can reside in the file system, on hard drives, on optical media, or almost anywhere your system can access. So where do these archive objects come from? SAP out of the box comes with numerous archiving objects (e.g. financial documents – FI_DOCUMNT). The archiving object defines the tables and their relationships so the customer can decide exactly what to archive. Once archived, the data is usually no longer visible in the system. There are ways to programmatically read back archived data as if it was still in the database but the transaction or process will have to be programmed as such. Using the archive browser, the customer could still view the archived files and data. In summary, the archiving mechanism is a very useful tool to fight data growth. Every SAP implementation must keep archiving in mind. The sooner that is considered, the easier it will be to execute.

Data Temperature

So, what if the data you need is not technically business complete and cannot be archived? What else can one do besides buying bigger HANA appliances? With later versions of HANA, the concept of data aging was introduced. Data records can be tagged as *hot, warm,* or *cold.* Hot means accessed recently. Cold means seldom touched. Warm lies in between. Not every piece of data is data aging enabled in S/4. But with each new release, more and more data has *aging capabilities.* So, what does aging do? It provides the system

---

[33] Relational Database Management System
[34] Database Administrator

information as to the frequency of access. This way, one can better manage and utilize the hardware. Memory is expensive. Hard drives are cheaper. While HANA is marketed as an *in-memory database*, the fact of the matter is that it can store data in traditional hard drives like before. This is where aging can help. By moving less accessed data to slower and cheaper media, it allows the in-memory portion of HANA to be *slim* and *trim* thus putting off the *high cost* of upgrades. A side benefit of data aging is that it also makes data access more efficient since there is *less data* to read thru. As an alternative, HANA tables can also be partitioned using a date to provide some "temperature" driven data storage splits.

Chapter III – Enterprise Structure

"Content without the context of business process is meaningless." Dennis Howlett.

An enterprise structure is the set of *foundational master data,* such as company, company code, controlling area, credit control area, functional area, consolidation business area and many other foundational elements that support your SAP system. In SAP, as in many other ERPs, once the organizational structure has been configured and transactions have posted, it is similar to "pouring concrete" on a foundation. Possible to change, but not an easy change for sure, requiring a significant amount of work.

Criticality of the Enterprise Structure

One of the key decisions and foundational blocks of any SAP Finance, or basically of *any* SAP implementation is the definition of the *Enterprise Structure* in the system. Designing the appropriate structure not only for how the business is structured today, but how it *might be* structured in the future is quite a challenging objective. In general, it is best to follow the principle of:

"You can always add two different sets of data, but it is much more difficult, and sometimes even impossible to subtract two sets of data"

To illustrate this concept, let's say you structure company code ABCD to represent your company's U.S. Operations and represent a legal entity for that customer. What happens if further down the road your customer would like to sell a regional portion of the business, say California operations? How would you be able to subtract those operations financial transactions and provide financial statements just for California operations and the rest of the U.S.? You could use cost centers to arrive at the tax jurisdiction code. However, if known in advance, potentially two company codes or more could have been setup in SAP, with ABCD being all U.S. Operations with CALI company code being the California operations. Once it comes to a divestiture transaction, carving out the California operations would be significantly easier. This is where that principle comes from, it is always easier to *add two sets* of data together (California plus rest of the U.S. together) than to try to *carve out* after the fact California operations from the rest of the U.S.

Key Components of the Enterprise Structure

There are several components of the enterprise structure when conducting an SAP implementation, among which are[35]:

- Chart of Accounts
- Controlling Area
- Company Code
- Business Area
- Functional Area
- Plant Code

Chart of Accounts

For most companies upgrading or *converting* from a prior financial system, it would be quite difficult or almost *next to impossible* to be able to a switch to an *entirely new* chart of accounts. If you have the opportunity to implement a *brand-new* chart of accounts, it is quite an imperative to design a chart of accounts that takes advantage of core SAP functionality. For a new COA implementation, it is best to try to avoid basing the design too much on a prior GL account system of a *non-SAP system*. Many SAP charts of accounts that are designed based on a prior *non-SAP system* will typically encounter the following challenges:

- Having redundant GL accounts, such as GL accounts that display a certain type of costs as opex[36], SG&A[37] or capital. In a SAP system, this cost classification will be captured by additional elements in a posting, such as cost center, cost center category, functional area, internal order, WBS element and many others.

- Increase the complexity of postings, such as having multiple GL accounts for sales transactions, causing confusion at time of posting for manual documents or creating *a quite complex interface logic* to select the appropriate GL account at the time of document posting.
  - For example, say in the prior non-SAP financial system, the company would have 1 GL account per type of product being sold, this should *not* be replicated in SAP, since SAP has other data elements that can be used to record a sales

---

transaction[38] and still achieve the same result recorded for that *single sale transaction* without duplicative master data.

- Create significant *on-going* master data challenges by having to create *new GL accounts* to fit in new accounting scenarios or for every new product or business line that arises, instead of relying on functionality from other SAP modules (such as SD or MM).

New Chart of Accounts Considerations

Following are potential questions to think about for a *brand-new* chart of accounts setup:

- Is the chart of account *logically grouped* into sets of structured accounts? For example, are all asset accounts in a *predictable range*, say 100'000'000 to 199'999'999?

- Are all the accounts the *same number* of digits?

- Do any of the accounts rely on having a leading zero? It is best to avoid leading zero for any of the accounts.

- Do the number ranges account for *future growth* of accounting requirements? In particular since in S/4 HANA *secondary cost elements* are GL accounts, does the proposed number range allow the inherent growth in *settlements, distributions* and other cost accounting requirements that require unique cost elements be created? Allow yourself future room for growth in needed cost elements.

- Is the numbering scheme *intuitive* and easy to memorize? For example, can users tell from *just looking* at the *very first digit* which type of account it is?

- Can the users easily identify what an account is representing? For example, just by knowing the first few digits, can the user identify *where* in the income statement or balance sheet that transaction will be presented? For example, if a GL account is 120'000'000, does the first digit convey that fact that it is an asset account? What about the second digit? Perhaps it represents accounts receivable?

- Are the accounts easily differentiable from one another? In other words, avoid reusing the same digit so that users can tell from the first digit the main type of account (asset, liability, equity, revenues, expenses, taxes, depreciation, etc....)

- For secondary cost elements, now *GL accounts in S/4 HANA*, is the design intuitive enough to understand cost flows? For example, does

---

[38] For example, material number and the associated hierarchy of material group, unit of measures, etc...

a sequence of digits identify what constitutes a *settlement transaction* vs. what constitutes a *distribution transaction*? What about for capital settlements? Does the cost element design allow for other elements embedded to easily recognize *from* and *to* cost flows? For example, the number 7 in the middle of the account may identify costs within an operating plant vs. number 8 which may identify costs allocated *from* corporate operations?

- Would this chart of accounts be flexible enough to fulfill future accounting requirements? In other words, how many total combinations could be created with the proposed account ranges?
- When designing a new chart of accounts, are you taking advantage of other financial master data that creates flexibility, such as the functional area, cost center category or designations of capital expense vs. operating expenses?
  - As an example, say a GL account is labeled "Consulting Services". Instead of creating a specific accounting for "Consulting Services Expense" and another GL account for "Consulting Services Capital" make sure you are factoring in additional dimensions used by SAP financials (in this case cost objects).
- For creating the GL account long-text, do you have a defined strategy and naming convention? For example, the long text of a GL account may not allow for the full description of an account, e.g. shortening *Cost of Goods Sold* to *COGS* might allow more consistent naming. Having this naming convention in advance, agreed upon by all key stakeholders and widely understood will be critical for a successful implementation of a new SAP chart of accounts.

Migrating from an already defined SAP Chart of Accounts
If the project you are working on is migrating from an *existing* SAP system, there are several considerations to take into account from a Chart of Accounts perspective. The following questions are food for thought when completing this type of project:

- If completing a *greenfield* project, does the current COA in the client's SAP system have a numbering allotment *sufficient* for current and future growth? Also, with the change in S/4 HANA Finance to cost elements being GL accounts, it is important to have enough number ranges available to accounts for need for CO settlements, distributions and other activity.

- Is the company looking to expand into foreign markets, acquire other companies and grow aggressively in the future? Remember that for each *single bank account* that a company has, a unique GL account must be setup to facilitate bank account reconciliations and banking interfaces[39].

- Particularly for greenfield projects taking advantage of Central Finance functionality, does the new S/4 HANA COA allow opportunities to expand the chart of accounts, say by adding a prefix or suffix to the existing chart of accounts in the new system? That way when postings are replicated in the new S/4 Central Finance systems, they would be converted to the new Chart of Accounts.

Controlling Area

The controlling area is the *highest level* organizational unit within the CO module. All cost objects within the CO module must be assigned directly to a *single* controlling area. For example, a cost center can only be assigned to a company code, and subsequently a company code can only be assigned to one controlling area.

The need to setup *multiple* controlling areas must evaluated very closely. There are several implications for setting up another controlling area, since it will impact multiple modules, including Controlling, Project Systems, Plant Maintenance, Maintenance Module, HR module, and many others. Use cases for setting up more than one controlling area:

- The company codes under the additional controlling areas will be treated as *non-consolidated entities* and typically cannot have intercompany transactions, but instead will be treated as *related party*.

- Are there legal or statutory requirements in a particular jurisdiction that extensively reviews cost settlements or distributions from the parent company or affiliated company? If so, it might be prudent to setup additional controlling areas to provide this *easily auditable* process between different companies.

- Remember that postings between the controlling area cannot be systematically be posted inside SAP[40], therefore, some

---

[39] This may potentially change with newer versions of SAP S/4 HANA. As of the time of this writing, SAP has plans to simplify this requirement and potentially may no longer require the same GL account to bank account relationship. For more information, visit
https://blogs.sap.com/2020/10/07/highlights-for-finance-in-sap-s-4hana-2020/

[40] Just to clarify that this refers to out of the box functionality. Of course, the system could be customized or an external tool be used to transfer costs between controlling areas.

customization or interface work will be required for cost postings that *cross* controlling areas.

- Where does the reporting line of sight occur? Do all the departments or group ultimately report to one key executive? By having a *single* controlling area and a standard cost center hierarchy, which allows for *consolidating* and *reporting* costs all the way from the *lowest level* in the organization to the *highest level*. Cost reporting becomes significantly easier with a single controlling area. This is an area to keep in mind if the customer implementing SAP has a highly centralized organization. For more decentralized business units or reporting structure, separate controlling areas might offer some advantages (for example by having allocations or settlements in local currency).

Company Code

SAP has historically defined a company code as being a *legal entity* requiring its own **fully balanced** set of financial statements[41] to meet statutory or external reporting requirements. The importance on this definition is quite relevant since for many clients around the world, this *very strict* definition may not necessarily be used or could be applied successfully.

Many clients have *internal reporting* requirements for having fully balanced set of financials *beyond* the legal entity concept. For example, a manager may be interested in having a cash flow statement for each division of the company, be able to analyze working capital by division and other requirements that that the pure *legal entity* definition does not provide. This is where the company code *branch* concept comes to the rescue.

The concept of company code *branches* or having a company code which is *not* a registered legal entity is widely used by many SAP customers. When using company code branches, a company would simply setup a new SAP company code to meet *primarily* internal financial reporting or consolidation needs. Say for example a manager would like to have a full set of financial statements, with a full balance sheet, for the 3 divisions under that manager. Three company codes could be setup to hold the entire assets, liabilities and equity of all 3 divisions. In addition, transactions among these 3 new company codes could be easily consolidated and sales & cost of goods sold

---

[41] Fully balanced includes balance sheet and income statement. Cash flow reporting is typically handled outside of "core" SAP, with consolidation applications such as SAP Business Planning & Consolidation (BPC) or Oracle Hyperion Financial Management (HFM).

eliminated to showcase only *third-party* sales for these 3 divisions, and not sales *between* these divisions.

Although there are significant improvements made by SAP over the past couple of years in terms of *Document Splitting*[42] functionality, many companies simply have not fully relied on document splitting to produce a fully balanced set of books for *external reporting*. There are still many challenges with document splitting for complex transactions such as balance sheet only entries, cash receipts or cash applications and other scenarios. In addition, many external consolidation or reporting systems, such as Oracle Hyperion Financial Management, rely primarily on the concept of having company code setups, since it can be assured that all transactions between company codes will usually have trading partner and other elements required for successful elimination of *intra-company* and *inter-company* transactions for sales and cost of goods sold.

Disadvantages of Company Code Branches

Although many corporations use company code branches, they do come with several potential disadvantages:

- Typically, all kinds of external or legal relationships would only be available for a legal entity, not for branches. For example, a bank account *can only be* opened for a corporate legal entity, not for a company code or division of a legal entity.

- Having branches can complicate tax and other regulatory reporting since many branches have to now be consolidated into a single reportable or taxable entity. Depending on the tax compliance[43] or consolidation[44] solution, trying to consolidate all the different types of transactions and still keep a *legal entity* vs. *branch* view can become quite burdensome.

- Can increase the complexity and frequency of master data setups for other critical modules, such as Sales & Distribution, Materials Management and Plant Maintenance. For example, every time a division or department is organized or re-organized, new branches

---

[42] Document splitting, in a summary, is a functionality that theoretically allows a customer to have full set of financial statements at the segment, profit center, business area and many other elements. It is still an evolving functionality as of the time of this writing, with some challenges particularly with balance sheet only transactions.

[43] For example, CorpTax, one of the largest income tax compliance applications in the market, similarly relies on a legal entity view for Tax compliance purposes.

[44] As discussed previously, solutions such as Oracle HFM, although they can technically consolidate on master data such as profit center or business area, some of the data quality may not be reliable enough to be able reliably present fully consolidated financial statements.

will have to be setup and impact master and transactional data in the very business-critical logistics modules. For example, new plant codes and plant maintenance data transactional records will have to be migrated to new plant codes linked to new company codes. This can become quite burdensome if a client is used to having department reorganizations and would like to have this line of sight for operations from a branch company code view.

Business Area

SAP's vision on Business Area, although supported for the time being, is generally advising clients to *not rely* on business area since no new developments are expected to happen in the business area space[45]. A business area can cross multiple company codes. A business area can be input directly on the transaction, but most typically is derived from the cost center[46]. A business area is usually implemented for internal reporting purposes and more or less a full set of financial statements can be generated. For example, externally a company may group its business units into segments such as Refining, Marketing and Midstream. For internal purposes, business areas can be created that cross these segments and report on it from a geographical perspective (e.g. US West Coast, US Central Region, Europe Northwest, Europe South and so forth). That way internal reporting can be at a *much more granular basis* than for external reporting purposes.

Functional Area

Functional Area within FI allows a company to organize business operations and departments for *Cost of Sales* Accounting purposes. The functional area concept allows a company to view costs from an *organizational type* perspective. For example, *Administration* can be a functional area, or *Sales* could be another area. For a multi-national company, the customer would be able to know *how much* of the total costs are administration costs or sales support costs *regardless* of which company code or cost center these costs sit in.

Functional area, if well implemented and designed, can be one of the most value-adding features of SAP Finance as it allows a company to have a *multidimensional* view of costs. Cost objects can be assigned to a functional area such as cost center or WBS elements, so for example an organization can know how much administrative-type projects (regardless of capital or

---

[45] https://blogs.sap.com/2019/03/13/business-area-in-sap-s4hana-sap-central-finance-cfin/
[46] https://help.sap.com/viewer/6a49d1604ffc4b908f9f78fba3824187/6.17.17/en-US/239fc2531bb9b44ce10000000a174cb4.html

expense) are costing the company. The same for other functional areas being setup such as IT, Finance, Human Resources and other functions.

Profit Center Structure

Profit Centers are an essential master data element in SAP, and one of the elements relied in Document Splitting to balance each financial entry. The definition of profit center in an implementation is as important as the definition of Company Code, since the profit center is a balancing characteristic and any change or migration to a new profit center would almost be treated as a company code consolidation or migration. A profit center, as a master data element, can provide an almost fully balanced set of books. Additionally, profit centers are tightly integrated into the logistics modules such as Sales & Distribution, Materials Management and many others. For example, profit center determination relies on plant code transactions and is derived through a complex logic to arrive at the right *profit center* from say a sales order. The same with inventory in materials management for product costs.

When implementing a profit center structure, it is important to understand that having the right number of profit centers fundamental. Have too few, and reporting lacks details, have too many (i.e. one profit center per customer) and reporting becomes almost impossible to aggregate.

Below we have formulated a couple of sample questions to think about when *creating* or *defining* a profit center:

- What is the organization's expectation from profit center accounting reporting?
- What types of metrics or KPIs is the company expected to use profit centers for?
- Will these metrics be only for income statement or also for select balance sheet metrics such as working capital, inventory calculations and others?
- How stable is the current company and have there been recent re-organizations inside the company? What are some of the pain points experienced during those re-organizations?
- Would the organization be defining a profit center as a product or series of products that will be fairly stable and will have a *low probability* of being re-organized or split in the future?
    - o   For example, for a Petroleum Refining company, perhaps defining profit center as supply locations would make sense,

assuming they are setup at the lowest level possible. For example, the customer could create sales areas or fuel value chains where fuels are sold and those could represent profit centers. This setup could allow end-users to further understand profitability from a regional or value chain perspective, regardless of which company code each refining, logistics or marketing assets sits on.

- o Another perspective for a company, if the company's group of products are fairly stable, the customer might be able to setup a profit center as groups of products or a regional combination. Continuing the refining company example, the company could setup profit centers based on "motor unblended gasoline" "or on-road diesel"

- o A combination could be setup, for example, "U.S. West Coast Gasoline profit center", which would encompass all the transactions necessary to *produce, inventory, transport, market* and *sell* one gallon of gasoline in the U.S. West Coast region.

- Define the *minimum* and *maximum* limit of profit centers taking into account other characteristics in other modules within SAP.

- o For example, it would not make sense to setup a profit center to be a customer since other elements like customer number or business partner are already used in FI. Even other modules outside FI, like Sales & Distribution or CRM provide extensive reporting in the customer space.

- o Some organizations decide to *mirror* their cost center structure and have a profit center per cost center. This is generally not advisable since the profit center would lose its *aggregative* features and become very difficult to report on. Imagine a sales analyst trying to shift through hundreds of thousands of profit centers on an Analysis for Office report, which would impact the performance of the report.

- o Opposite of that, having a 1 single profit center per organization structure would violate the first principle discussed in the chapter, *it is easier to add data than to subtract.*

- It is generally not advisable to assign a profit center to a single company code, instead allowing to cut across company codes as it enables a powerful reporting capability beyond what has been setup as a company code entity or branch.

Segment

Segment reporting was launched by SAP in the mid 2000's, right around with document splitting functionality in the "New GL" series of product upgrades for ECC 6.0. Since many customers still remain in the "Classic GL" version of GL, segment is not as widely used in ECC 6.0. For S/4 HANA Finance, since New GL and document splitting are enabled by default, many customers should carefully review and understand the benefits of using segment reporting. Segment reporting arose due to both the FASB and IFRS[47] Foundation updating their accounting principle standards requiring *segment-level* disclosures for external financial reporting.

A segment is defined at the profit center and similar to business area can also be manually selected when posting financial transactions in GL. A segment allows the ability to create a balance sheet and income statement at this level. As per SAP documentation, more and more functionality is being added over time to the Segment element and away from business area. In fact, the default recommendation by SAP, is to use segment instead of business area[48]. Potentially both the business area and segment could be combined to provide additional dimensions to report on (for example have Segment represent key products while having business area represent a geographical view).

Plant Code

A plant code is the highest organizational unit in the Logistics module, such as Sales & Distribution, Materials Management, Plant Maintenance and many others. A plant code is typically defined in terms of a *physical location* where operations take place. For example, a refinery could be considered a plant code since the activities performed take place in a *finite physical area* or space. The same with materials management as well and sales & distribution. For example, a section of a pipeline could be defined as a plant code since products are shipped through that pipeline in a defined physical space.

Challenging scenarios for Plant Codes

There are some complex scenarios to consider when setting up plant codes:

- What about for trading operations, where trading may be transacted in terms of paper operations and not a physical receipt or delivery point?

---

[47] Financial Accounting Standards Board and International Financial Reporting Standards foundation, are the two largest accounting standard setting organizations. FASB oversees U.S. Generally Accepted Accounting Principles while IFRS oversees the international accounting standards.

[48] https://help.sap.com/viewer/17ec785ed2294431b933daf9a926af80/6.17.17/en-US/6b63c7531dc61d4be10000000a174cb4.html

- What about when a facility has *multiple ownership* or joint ventures within the same facility? For example, in a refinery, say besides the main fuels production areas, it has chemical co-located facilities owned by a separate legal entity, how would the customer address the separate reporting since a plant code can only be assigned to one company code?

- For example, if a company were to form a joint venture or sell a portion of the refinery to a different owner, how would they address the separation of plant codes without impacting critical operations that would occur *regardless* of company code structure or ownership considerations?

- Always consult with logistics experts within the client's IT department and engage operations and sales organizations as to design plant codes and company code structures with their goals in mind as well, not simply from a financial reporting structure. Remember a company's purpose is not *solely* to provide internal or external financial reporting, but to actually conduct operations, repair equipment, sell products and purchase materials or feedstocks.

Consider the present but also the future

Say if tomorrow your company were to be required to report financial statements from a different perspective, is the enterprise structure flexible enough and created at the *lowest* possible granular level to facilitate ease of change? We would venture to say that most organizations' enterprise structures *are not* flexible enough to be able to accommodate these re-organization changes. Consider as well the impacts to systems *outside* of SAP, like financial consolidations systems, banking, and many others. Can these reporting changes be made in your SAP system without impacting to day-to-day operations in these other systems? Remember always to keep in mind the key principle outlined before, that it is possible to *add data*, but much more difficult to *subtract* from an aggregate level of detail to a *lower level* of detail.

Impacts to financial statements

Having a company code branch structure at the *lowest level possible* allows the company to flexibly reorganize or restructure segment reporting by using a system not extensively linked to other pieces of master or structure in SAP. For example, if your entire financial reporting is built based on company codes adding up to a reportable segment, this would provide the ultimate flexibility instead of having to restructure and create new company codes, profit centers etc… each time an organization change is made. This would also minimize the impacts to logistics, such as having to create or change plant codes and all the massive master and transactional data associated with a plant code in modules such as plant maintenance[49].

Internal Reporting structures

As mentioned in the prior pages, be sure to take advantage of structures like profit center segment, functional area for costs, elements within SD like Sales Organizations or Divisions, or profit center reporting to be able to supply *granular* and *applicable* reporting structures. For example, say a refining operations VP wants to know the sales of *all gasoline* products *across all the refineries* in the company, do you have a segment for motor gasoline sales already established or a grouping of profit centers created? Having these types of hypothetical questions would allow to weigh in during the implementation the pros and cons of each element selected.

Comparison of structures

It is important to understand the uses of the different elements of financial master data and structure. The following table attempts to compare the different elements between whether they should be used for *external reporting* or *internal reporting:*

Element	External Reporting	Internal Reporting
Company Code	Yes	Yes
Segment	*Potentially* with some caveats.	Yes, crosses company codes
Business Area	*Potentially, not recommended for future implementations*	Yes, but limited
Profit Center	Not fully, some challenges in document splitting	Yes, very powerful as it crosses company codes
Plant Code	No	Yes
Functional Area	No	Yes, only for costs

---

[49] As an example, a plant code will have a functional location, equipment, equipment records, bill of materials, associated with a plant code. It is always recommended to engage the IT group in charge of logistics as to not create unintended consequences and higher costs *upstream* of financial reporting.

Technical Point of View

Plan, plan, plan. It would seem that planning is key to a successful SAP implementation especially when dealing with enterprise structures. Without a crystal ball, how could one plan for the future? Making the right choices for a transitional or migration project seems straight forward. Leaving enough room to expand and grow is the trickier part – but at what cost?

Number Ranges Explained

Many enterprise master / configuration entities may be setup to utilize a number range. What is a number range? Think of it as an auto incrementing construct. Via configuration, some entities allow for "external" and "internal" numbering / naming. With external, you can freely name the entity as you see fit (provided it's not already used) AND it fits within the semantic definition of that particular entity. Semantic definition merely refers to the technical definition – is a numeric, alphanumeric, etc. One cannot use an alpha character in the name/numbering of an entity which requires numbers only.   In contrast, internal numbering is when the system will generate a number for the entity during creation. Via config, some configuration is allowed for this range (i.e. starting number, ending number). Both external and internal schemes can be utilized to implement "smart naming" as previously recommended. Some areas of configuration allow the customer to assign a portion of a number range to specific groupings.   For example, a sales document number may be 10 digits long but via configuration, one could segment it off and have it based on document type. Sales orders may start with 1 million thru 1,999,999. Transfers may start with 2 million thru 2,999,999. Keep in mind that as time goes on, the maximum amount can be reached so one generally wants to leave enough room. Some number ranges allow for a "year" designation. Basically, this type of number range resets for each of the years specified. A perfect example would be FI documents. FI documents can be configured to start over with doc number 1 at the beginning of each fiscal year. This way, the possibility of running out of document numbers would be minimized.

Number Range Buffering

One unique feature of number ranges is that it can be buffered (if intended). Imagine if internal numbering is configured. This means that during the creation of an entity (or a document), the system will automatically assign the "next" number to that newly created item. The system has to guarantee that no two items will get the same number for uniqueness purposes. In technical terms, this is what one would consider single threading. Only one process can dispense these numbers to assure no duplicates are handed out. This single threading presents a huge bottleneck. To combat this, number ranges can be buffered (not all are designed to – this is driven by the application which uses the number range). Buffering merely means getting some numbers in advance. Via this method, several processes can hand out numbers because each has requested a "buffer" of numbers. One may have 11 thru 20. Another may have 21 thru 30. So on and so forth. This way, when processes request a new number, dependent upon which service responds to that request, they will get either a number within the teens or the twenties. But none will be repeated ultimately. Moreover, all numbers should theoretically be used up with no gaps (more on this later). One a process has handed out all the previously requested buffered numbers, it'll request the next set (e.g. 31 thru 40). This type of buffering scheme is known as *main memory buffering*. The numbers are held in memory for fast access to maximize performance. Is there a drawback? Of course. Memory is *volatile*. If someone accidentally *disconnects* the server, those numbers are gone (i.e. not used because next time it'll request the next block). So main memory buffering can lead to gaps. *Do not use* this type of buffering scheme if you must have *no gaps* in the numbering. For those extreme situations whereby no gaps are allowed, parallel buffering is available. Of course, one can always choose no buffering which would solve the problem of never having gaps at the expense of performance due to single threading. Parallel buffering is different in that it basically holds the *buffered numbers* in memory AND the *database*. It's not as fast as main memory buffering but if has the advantage that once a number is used, it'll be marked as used in that buffer. Next time the system comes back up, it'll pick up where it left off. In summary, each buffering scheme offers advantages and disadvantages. Choose wisely given the scenario.

Shape Matters

Are your enterprise structures setup to be wide and flat? Or narrow and tall? Why would that matter? Of course, the business requirements should drive this decision. However, one should always keep in mind the other side of the coin, the technical implications. SAP allows for many different ways to setup ones' data structures. For example, cost centers and profit centers can be organized as hierarchies. Doing so allows a lot of reporting and functional aggregation. This unfortunately comes at the cost of performance. Prior to S/4, hierarchy traversal was by far one of the biggest speed hogs. Any process that required processing at every node of a hierarchy often led to undesirable runtimes. With HANA being an in-memory database, much effort has been placed into speeding up the traversal of such hierarchies. Regardless, if the idea is to traverse from a node (e.g. cost center) upwards to the root (top cost center), shape matters. If the hierarchy structure is relatively flat, the process may only have to visit a very small number of parent nodes. As the hierarchy gets "taller" and "taller", the more time it'll take for that process to complete. Just like a tree, hierarchies need to be *pruned*. Keeping hierarchies clean improves overall performance as well as general usability.

Once You Start, You Can't Stop

Emphasizing planning again, SAP is great at giving the customer *many options* to setup the system. But once the system is live and data is actually stored in relation to those enterprise structures, it is a Herculean task to *change it*.

Case study: An oil and gas company acquired another company. Logic would dictate that a new "company code" would be setup for this new entity for financial analysis. However, the state is requiring that their severance tax reports be reported under the SAME company or tax payor. This presents a very difficult situation whereby if that was the prevailing requirement, one would integrate the new financials into the existing company thus allowing the report to work as it does now (just with more data). But then there could be no separation of analysis or reporting between the *original* company and the *acquired* company. In this particular situation, the SAP client actually chose to create a *new company code* but modified the severance tax report to consolidate the reports of *both company codes* into one report. It was something the standard SAP software could not handle. Moral of the story? There is no one perfect answer sometimes. But keep in mind that the decision made has a long-lasting effect. As previously stated, if it was decided to not create a new company code, it may be very difficult in the future to split up the data in the system and follow a different enterprise structure.

The Crystal Ball

Not quite a crystal ball but a tool which can help you if you didn't have one, SAP for years has had software which eased transformation and consolidation of master data. Master Data Governance[50] (originally called MDM - Master Data Management), is one such tool. It was originally designed to aid customers consolidate master data from multiple sources (e.g. legacy systems or acquired systems). It attempts to enforce the concept of

---

[50] For more information about MDG, visit https://www.sap.com/products/master-data-governance.html

one source of truth. A cost center object should be recognized in a specific way regardless of where it came from to the entire organization. Note that MDG is not simply a module like FI or CO. It is a complete software installation with its own hardware and software requirements. It requires an established *project* to implement and *on-going support* is required. In short, treat it like another SAP system. While the applicable situations for MDG is clear, it is something any mature SAP installation may have to consider *eventually.* So, don't count it out.

Chapter IV – End to End Testing

"The first comprehensive picture of whether the accounting numbers balance and make sense will arise during the month end process." Stephen Harwood.

Different types of testing

In a typical IT implementation, there are several stages of testing cycles, such as *IT testing*, *End-User testing* and *Integrated testing*. These different cycles of testing for an SAP implementation can be quite time consuming but are required to *reduce the risk* of the implementation, particularly trying to avoid *major* defects *during* or *after* an SAP go-live. These different stages of testing require careful planning, high degree of collaboration between the IT function and end-users as well the creation of comprehensive test scenarios. Striking a balance between covering all the *possible* scenarios and the time and effort it takes needs to be evaluated carefully and unfortunately there's no single solution (i.e. testing *everything* is not economically feasible).

IT Testing

In IT testing, testing is done by the IT department, typically either the IT SAP functional analyst or the IT SAP programmer or developer. The focus on IT testing is usually *program integrity* and the testing is not so much focused on *data integrity* at this stage in the process. What this type of testing seeks to do is as follows:

- Does the program work as *expected?* Of course, this expectation is based on the customer requirements as *understood* by the IT team, which could very well be *different* than what the user *actually* wanted to have built in the first place.
- Does the program *populate data* as expected or does it create errors?
- Minimal data checks are performed in this step (i.e. data is populated, not 100% certain whether it might be *valid business data* or not)
- Do calculations work as *expected* per the ABAP code or the design document?
- Does the program perform *reasonably* well in terms of runtimes? Please note that depending on availability of testing data in the development or acceptance environment, the *true test* for performance for a custom program will in many times be in a *productive environment.*

- Does the user selection screen or user interface conform to what the user specified in the business requirement or design document?
- Does the program *crash* or create an ABAP error when running certain combinations of data? What about if invalid values are entered?
- Does the output of the program conform to what the customer specified in discussions with the IT team?

End-User Testing

This is a type of testing done by end-users or *proxies* for the end-users. At this stage in the SAP implementation, many of the major bugs and issues should have been solved by the IT teams, but many issues potentially still remain. Particularly, since IT is focused on *fixing issues* and is not responsible *necessarily* for the integrity or *quality of data*, there will be many issues found within the user testing phase, particularly if there has been a *very long cycle* between requirements gathering and an actual demo or prototype. If possible, always try to minimize the cycle between requirements gathering and the first demo, the earlier the better as to gather valuable feedback from users.

End-user testing seeks to answer the following questions:

- Does the functionality perform as expected?
- Are there potential internal controls gap with this functionality? (i.e. letting an account reconciliation preparer *reconcile* and *approve* the same account)
- Are the calculations performed by this program as *expected?*
- Is data integrity maintained as expected from initial impressions?
- Is the runtime for this program acceptable to the user? Keep in mind that probably the demo will be done with *limited test data*, so if runtimes are a concern in the demo, be prepared for slower runtime once productive data is read by the program.
- Is the data easy to export to Microsoft Excel[51] or other software for reporting?
- Are the *inputs* and *outputs* of this program impacting somebody else or are the results *independent?* If the output of this report to be used by a downstream process, is the output in the right format?

---

[51] By default, SAP provides Microsoft Excel export capabilities on all programs, but the most user friendly is ALV or Automatic List View, which with a couple of clicks all data viewed on the program can be exported to Excel for further analysis.

- Is the program design easy to follow by the user or does it require very complex sequencing for execution?

Different types of testing

Just as there are different *cycles* of testing, there are also different *types* of testing. Those are *unit testing, iterative testing, user testing* and *integrated testing*.

Unit Testing

Unit Testing focuses on testing *individual portions* of a program or report, looking to validate whether that particular program or section of the program works as expected. Unit tests are typically performed by the IT function, by either the actual ABAP developer or an IT analyst with a functional SAP background. The main focus is not so much on the entire functionality of the program, but specifically *how the different* parts of the program work, thus why the name is called *unit* testing. For example, say a program is supposed to perform 2 steps, the first one is to display all the cost centers in the state of Texas. The second step or functionality is to display all the costs recorded for a specific year in the state of Texas. The first unit test would validate that the program's output matches up with the source table (in this example, the cost center table or CSKS) and the calculations are right (right number of Texas cost centers). The second unit test will ensure that the *actual financial postings* displayed in the program match up with ACDOCA for the specific period.

Iterative Testing

The process of iterative testing is an *incremental approach* to testing. Instead of doing a large unit testing at all once, it might help to start with a small prototype to understand how the data flows, and from there start building incremental additions to test out new functionality added in to the report or program. Additionally, once the program is stable, additional incremental changes will be made, tested and then continue programming to ensure base functionality works as intended. Another benefit of iterative testing is that might allow the IT analyst to better understand the *underlying data* and find potential gaps in the data and needed changes in the program. For example, let's say an assumption was made that *all cost centers* in Texas would start with TX followed by a number. The program might discover that this rule does not apply 100% of the time so that programmatic changes may have to occur before *releasing* the program to the user for further testing.

User Testing

As the name implies, this is testing done by the ultimate *end-user*, and it is typically a lot more *in-depth than* unit testing. One of the key outcomes of end-user testing is for the IT team to have further changes or inputs into the program. The more *frequent* and *incremental* the testing performed by end-users is, the higher quality the end-product will be. There is nothing more challenging for IT teams to build a solution with limited end-user testing and at the end of a *very long* development, many if not of all the user requirements have been completely missed, not well documented by the user or misinterpreted by the IT team. The more frequent and iterative user testing, the *lower number* of surprises there will be at the end of the development.

Integrated Testing

Integrated testing is more complex and it is applicable only where processes have a dependency or *predecessor* and/or *successor* relationships documented and in place. For example, the majority of independent reports (i.e. no process is dependent on the processing or output of data from the report being tested) fall under the category of having predecessor relationship with few or non-existing successor relationships (other processes depending on the output of these reports). The *higher* the number of successor processes depending on the changes or programs being implemented, the more *rigorous* the integrated testing should be. For example, if a new program is being changed that will generate thousands of financial postings, for which other programs use those postings as the input, the level of integrated testing should be *much higher* than for a *read-only* report that is used by a single user.

Determining areas for testing

There are several ways of determining which areas to test, but a good approach is to focus on the most *business-critical* processes for testing. Following are potential questions to think about during the planning phase for testing:

- What business processes generate the highest amount of data?
- What business processes have more interaction with an outside party? It is one thing to have an issue with an *internal* customer, but *external* customers are less forgiven and issues with those customers could expose the company to *contractual, reputation* or *legal* risks.
- What business process takes the *longest to run* during the month-end close or other critical finance activity? By focusing on this process, early indications of performance could increase the focus of the project on issues ahead.
- What business process has the *highest impact* on the most *critical lead* time during close? In other words, what process, if they were to delay

the financial close, would not have an *alternative* backup plan? Sample financial processes that come to mind:

    o   Depreciation: depreciation needs to be kept at a very low-level of detail, the asset level, which particularly in S/4, requires a large number of data to be processed for the entire process to be completed. Depreciation calculations in general do not have a backup plan (unless some sort of high level financial accrual or estimate postings are done). The other reason why depreciation is so critical, is that for most companies using the *indirect method* for cash flow calculations (primarily banks use the direct method), depreciation is the largest *non-cash* expense to transform from *accrual* accounting to a standard cash flow report. It is critical that a process like depreciation be tested and particularly in S/4 to be *stress-tested* due to the ongoing data model changes in fixed assets[52].

    o   Inventory: for most goods-producing industries, the assessment of inventory is quite important since it impacts the calculation of *COGS or Cost of Goods Sold*, which directly impacts the margin and net income calculations of the financial statements. Depending on the complexity of the inventory, the number of items being sold, pricing complexity and many more, inventory accounting can be one of the most difficult business process to successfully execute. In addition, if inventory will be handled in SAP in the Materials Management module, additional tests should be planned in terms of *pricing* and *valuation*, since inventory calculations have a *large* financial impact.

- What business processes would, by definition, require a *very low level* of sub-ledger or account details?

    o   Customer receivables, in other words, for a company to be business it needs to maintain very detailed customer *account records* for the customer to be able to understand the activity on their account and be able to pay the receivable balance. Inability to produce these detailed customer activity records could materially impact a company and lead to lower sales,

---

[52] For additional details on how depreciation has changed from ECC 6.0 to S/4 HANA, see the following blog post: https://serioconsulting.com/blog/new-depreciation-posting-run-in-s-4hana/

uncollectible receivables leading to cash flow issues and many more.

o   Sales tax compliance and other type of *indirect taxes*[53], which typically need to be kept at the county or municipality level, creating millions of very detailed records for several years (also for audit compliance as well). The inability to comply with extensive sales tax regulations could subject the company to *large fines, penalties* and potential loss of *"license to operate"* in a particular jurisdiction.

- What business processes have a large financial component but *originate outside* of SAP Finance? These processes would warrant additional testing since they do not originate in core SAP finance functionality Missing additional fields or components would be highly impactful to many business processes. Some examples include:

  o   Payroll and HR postings, including payroll taxes, salaries and wages payable and others.

  o   Order to Cash, typically these would reside in either a combination of custom non-SAP processes or SD/MM module type activities.

  o   Plant maintenance, the interaction would primarily be through some sort of settlement processes (i.e. work order settlement) but there could be other dependencies as well to consider.

  o   Inventory management, key integration through cost and profit center accounting, materials management, inventory valuation, LIFO/FIFO accounting and many more.

  o   Industry-specific modules, such as those in the Oil & Gas industry such as *Production Revenue Accounting, Joint Venture Accounting,* or *Trader Supply Workbench* (TSW).

Importance of good scenarios for testing

As critical as *selecting the areas* for testing, it is even *more important* to select *comprehensive scenarios* to ensure testing provides a reasonable assurance that financial processes are working as *expected.* Planning comprehensive scenarios would minimize the risk of an issue not being detected as well potentially minimize testing that does not add value.

---

[53] Indirect tax is typically thought to encompass areas such as sales tax, excise tax, Value-Added Tax, and other types of taxes with the exclusion of income taxes.

Following are several questions that could be used during a testing planning implementation:

- How different are the business processes using the program or transaction to be tested?
    - For example, for a commonly used transaction you may have to build robust scenarios that at least encompass a good size of the most critical business processes. A good example in SAP Financials is transaction code FB01, which is used for manual financial postings. The combination of potential scenarios associated just with this transaction code could be quite large. Just testing the transaction with one scenario would not be enough to qualify as assurance that everything works as expected. Start thinking in terms of the different scenarios that should be created, such as revenue postings, cost postings, *intercompany* and *intracompany* postings, accruals, postings to WBS elements and many more.
- How commonly used is this transaction or report?
    - For most widely used transactions, since many analysts will be looking at it, it might make more sense to use the *most complex scenario* or set of testing and test the full process. Otherwise, users might be testing the *same* transaction with small variations of the data that do not yield a different result. In other words, if you are testing FB01 (posting an SAP entry), it does not matter if 1 cost center is selected or 1,000 cost centers are tested, the result will be the same. It might make more sense to select 1 cost center and WBS element instead to provide more variability of the results. Or testing the same financial entry with 10 different company codes might not be the best use of time or resources.
    - For less commonly used transactions, do they have a potential workaround if that transaction were *not to* work as expected? Could a user easily post a manual transaction if the original program were not to work?
- Is this transaction *creating/modifying* or *displaying records?* For those transactions *creating* data or records, it is more critical to have robust scenarios and test different types of *combinations* of data. Otherwise, data integrity could be at stake. Those programs displaying records,

particularly those that are independent reports, should have less focus in terms of testing vs. programs that create records. An additional consideration for programs that only display records is that they could potentially uncover issues *not with the program itself*, but with the data further upstream. Say a report displays intercompany transactions, the program would be perfectly ok, but should be tested to ensure that no other program or change has impacted *the data* that this program is using.

- Do you have available a list of *critical fields* that in the very end of the process, say in financial reporting, must have? Examples include:
  - o Trading Partner, which is used for consolidation and elimination of intercompany entries. Incorrect trading partners being posted would cause the company to *overstate* revenues and cost of goods since inter/intra company transactions would not be properly eliminated.
  - o Derived fields when posting, such as *business area* or *segment* that are used to present financial data at different levels in the organization.
  - o Are those fields posted with the transaction or derived through reporting from setups in the master data? A good example is functional area, which is not posted in the transaction, but held at the master data level in the cost center. Those that are not directly recorded in the financial transaction posted are easier to change, particularly if you are relying on applications *outside* of the ERP to consolidate financial results.

One possible testing strategy would be to pursue a *"dumbbell"* shape of scenarios. In other words, select or prepare the *most extreme* scenarios for testing, such as a *large set* of cost centers, a complex mixture of inputs and then select a simple one. In addition, in the middle do as little testing as possible since the assumption is that if *both simple* and *complex* scenarios are pursued, then there is *limited upside* or items to be found in pursuing a hybrid of medium complexity scenarios.

Start with the end in mind, Reporting

Reporting is usually one of the most overlooked areas for an SAP implementation and it is typically left towards the very end of the testing cycle when other processes have completed their testing. In our opinion, this is not a good approach, and the reporting deliverables should be addressed as early as possible in order to *influence* and *mitigate* any errors found during transactional data postings.

Focusing on reporting provides many advantages, such as:

- Since reporting is at the *very end* of *long* and *interconnected* financial processes and typically is tested at the very least, it is quite relevant to have the *end-reporting* in mind from the very beginning of the SAP implementation.

- Once several thousands or millions of records are *posted* or *created*, it is quite a herculean task to be able to fix those records in SAP. Have regular checkpoints with the financial reporting team along the way and provide *sample data* created from the various financial processes. Do not wait until the very end when most processes have finalized the development and testing phases.

- By having the *very end* of the process in mind, this can help with upstream process in coming up with good test scenarios. For example, if the most valuable field is *segment* for financial reporting, the other predecessor financial processes can focus on ensuring that the segment field carries through the entire financial close processes. It might help having a list of the critical *must-have fields* to ensure data integrity throughout the financial close process. This list should be shared with all the teams involved in financial processes, including those on the logistics side or feeder modules.

Integrated Testing – Month-End Close

Throughout many financial SAP projects, one of the key determinants of whether a project was successful in delivering value or no, is the *month-end close process* or MEC. The MEC, along with other end-processes like account reconciliations, is typically were the *majority* of business and financial processes come together to at the end of the accounting cycle to process payments, run depreciation, produce *reliable* financial statements and many other outcomes. In other words, each process in isolation would generally pass most unit tests, but the *sum of the parts* in coordination, the MEC, would be the ultimate test. Start discussions early around the sequencing and timing of MEC. Typically, you would like to have a minimum of 2 month-end close sequential tests, but more likely 3. The first MEC will take longer as there is significant coordination to ensure the sequencing goes right. The second one should go better and would allow to review the results of the first MEC. Additionally, the second MEC could be focused on measuring performance.

The third MEC should simulate conditions on a typical quarter-end close or a year-end close scenario where processes that are only run once are tested. By having a well-structured financial close process testing, you can exponentially increase the change of success of your SAP S/4 HANA Finance implementation.

Potential issues that could be encountered during the first couple of financial month-end closes:

- Has sequencing of the execution of processes been discussed by both the customer and IT team? Are all dependencies well understood?

- Start thinking *how* the month-end close would run the *first few months* after go-live. It is best to automate the sequencing and execution of processes *after a couple of months* to allow any adjustments in the schedule. Early automation may sound like a good idea, however in the first couple of months flexibility should be higher priority than automation.

- Does the amount of data being processed *reasonably* reflect what a *typical* month-end close would be? The amount of data should be in line with what a real-time production execution would be, otherwise the expected run times would be unrealistically too good to be true.

- Is the performance *between* processes acceptable to meet the business unit, corporate or even external financial reporting requirements and deadlines? While a process many have passed all the unit and end-user testing, low performance of one financial process may potentially delay further month-end close requirements down the road, impacting the entire financials implementation.

- While many of the inputs used in unit testing scenarios or user testing are typically posted or created *manually*, the inputs for most financial close processes would be created by *predecessor processes*, which is one of the key *benefits* of MEC testing but also one of the main *challenges*. Having comprehensive scenarios that simulate or preferably *mirror* those existing processes would provide a higher level of risk assurance than just posting a couple of manual entries and running them through the system.

- Is your implementation from an already existing SAP system or is it from a non-SAP system? If you have already an existing SAP system that you are upgrading, lots of *existing* data can be leveraged and re-posted to simulate what a typical month would be. If the project is being done from a non-SAP system, you should expect to allocate *more time* on planning the different scenarios and ensuring that those new scenarios will be reflected of the new SAP implementation.

- How are both *inbound* and *outbound* interfaces performing? Do they carry through successful postings and exchange data with the necessary interfaces? Another consideration is that if the existing systems that provide inbound or outbound data to the new SAP system will stay *as-is* or will they be *upgraded* to a new version or migrated to SAP. If they will stay *as-is*, then existing inputs and outputs could be replicated so this should reduce the complexity in scenarios. However, if these inbound or outbound applications are being moved to SAP logistics, additional time should be planned for testing the integration points. Generally, the more data points are integrated, the higher probability that issues would arise. In other words, a simpler FI posting interface from a third-party system is easier to test than a fully integrated MM/SD module interface with a trading application with many more data points.

- What are the back-end processes that would assure that all *necessary elements* for financial reporting are completed successfully? Is it account reconciliations? Is it customer reports for receivables or payments? Is it reporting on sales tax liabilities to the state? Has the MEC allowed enough time for these processes to review the output of the MEC? As a general rule, it is best to increase the level of focus on testing on business processes farther *downstream* from the originating financial transactions. The tax function typically has processes that sit at the very end of a series of financial processes and because of this, testing these tax processes can provide a wealth of testing possibilities and insights. If data has been processed and it is in good state for compliance and reporting of the different types of tax (sales tax, property tax, income tax, etc…), then this should raise the level of confidence that the state of project implementation is in a good shape.

  - o For example, when testing the order to cash and procure to pay businesses, having representation from sales and income tax individuals so that those groups can test reporting and payment of different types of taxes. Not only does this benefit the tax department but it benefits the entire implementation by providing much needed data validation.
  - o Another example would be to incorporate an analyst from the income tax area in any testing of financial depreciation.

In the U.S., and similar to other countries, income tax laws require companies to keep *very detailed* fixed asset records and provide for *different* depreciation useful lives, methodologies and much more, so it is a good idea to keep this group informed of changes and required testing. For example, once depreciation and other fixed assets processes run, have an analyst from this tax function validate the end-results. Potentially this test from the tax analyst could provide insights into incorrect data, incorrect configuration and program bugs. Early involvement from the tax function is key to a successful SAP finance implementation.

Flow through and simulation of year-end close

Although the first couple of month-end closes will probably be quite a change from the client's prior month-end close processes, simulating the year-end close is also a good practice before go-live that should not be *overlooked*.

During year-end close there are several processes that are only run once a year:

- Balance Carryforward, for both balance sheet and income statement accounts. This is important as testing it out early to figure out any data conversion issues, incorrect SAP configuration, potential SAP bugs and to understand the overall performance of how long it will take to run this yearly process.

- As part of securities regulations and reports such as the SEC 10K for a publicly traded company, the number of reports and disclosures required for year-end close purposes are quite larger than for regular quarter-end closes or just for internally disclosed month-end closes. This is why having at least a sample of what data these year-end reports will require is a good idea. For example, have the financial accounting/reporting or external reporting team provide all the required data inputs for successful reporting. With these inputs, trace them from the different reporting systems back to SAP transactions. Can your SAP implementation provide those data inputs to these customers or will there have to be some sort of manual adjustments in spreadsheets? The answer might be due to the complexity of calculations that it can only be manually provided, but at least all stakeholders will be aware in advance of the year-end close and plan accordingly. In addition, by providing mock or test reports, your team might be able to spot potential program bugs, data conversion or data transformation issues. As mentioned earlier, it is best to start with the end in mind.

- The execution of reports such as actuals vs. budget, actuals this quarter vs. last quarter and so forth can help identify potential issues in your implementation. For example, if sales the last quarter were $1 billion, but in the current test environment, after most or all transactions have been replicated, are $100 million, this should be a cause of concern and should be researched further.

- Account reconciliations is also another good financial process to test out for a variety of accounts. Keep in mind that certain GL accounts, as per the company's account policy, will only be reconciled once a year or once a quarter. It is generally a good idea to have a good mixture of monthly accounts, quarterly and even yearly accounts.

Technical Point of View

For every task in a project, there are degrees of *completeness* or acceptable *tolerances*. Technical testing is no exception. To expect every line of code to be tested would be unrealistic. A company's decision on the depth of technical testing can have vast impacts on timelines and budgets.

Test as You Go

With regards to custom development (which most SAP installations have or will have), the smallest error at the most basic foundation of a process could ripple issues up the chain. It is prudent to test as the development takes shape. With each iteration of the development, testing should be done to make sure the new functionality works as well as any existing functionality. This type of repetitive testing can be time consuming. Did SAP leave you high and dry? ABAP Units to the rescue! ABAP unit is a construct which SAP delivered many moons ago but requires a bit of dedication on the customer's part to take advantage of its benefits. The promise is that one can run ABAP unit tests in an automated fashion. This way, a developer can execute these previously written ABAP unit tests and it should theoretically verify that previous functionality still works as expected. Knowing this tool exists, why are ABAP units not more popular? Mainly because of its implementation. Your mileage may vary but the constraints are the same. In order to use ABAP units, the development you want to test must be written in ABAP objects.

For each method in your ABAP object, a corresponding ABAP unit test method can be created to basically "test" the method. The test cases are written just like any other ABAP code (with some special syntax). The test cases provide the input parameters and expected assertions (results). This in itself lies the big issue with ABAP units and the reason for its slow adoption. While software design and development style are not covered in this book – it is a universal truth that there are a million ways to code the same logic. Some developers prefer to create methods for every little operation. Some prefer to logically group them into business tasks. The *more* the class method does – the *less useful* ABAP unit test cases become. Unless the development is so decomposed into small operational methods, one cannot easily have created 100% coverage ABAP units for them. Moreover, ABAP units written for larger methods can lead to false negatives (i.e. hidden problems but test shows positive results). One can then easily say – our corporate development mandate is to write methods at the lowest level so we can take advantage of ABAP units. While that is idealistic, the *drawback* is that the development time will increase (more methods to write, more ABAP units to write) as well as performance could *suffer* since no block operations can be done – every operation has to be distilled down to the lowest level. So, take it for what it is. Great concept. Less than *perfect* real-world usage.

Think Bigger

If ABAP Units is not right for your company, are there other technical testing tools available out there? Test tools a plenty! While each has its own strengths and weaknesses, they are all based on the same premise of test cases which are repeatable. Cost/benefit of each is up to each customer to decide. Over a decade ago, SAP released TDMS (Test Data Management System) with limited success. The idea is to basically allow a customer to selectively pull out large chunks of data (generally based on some type of business criteria like a date) and later allows one to compare these. One major drawback to such a tool is that data may not exactly look the same but are semantically the same (e.g. two FI documents have different document numbers but were posting the same scenario and have the same financial and reporting impact). Moreover, larger processes (e.g. month end close) requires so much data that it became impractical to compare such not to mention the amount of database space required. TDMS was generally setup as a separate server from the main landscape so there are also hardware costs involved. In short, another miss.

So, What Now?

While there are tools out there which will minimize the effort of testing, there is *no way* of getting around *actually* putting in the work and time. Here are some key points and suggestions to ease the pain.

Test the norm and the extremes:

Testing the norm is what any regular test case would cover. From a technical point of view, the greatest frequency of failure would be the extremes (both low and high). Create abnormal test cases to stress the program and process with unusually *low* and *high* values. This will test the edge limits of the process and can reveal hidden issues which may not pop up until the system is live. Common errors could be *divide by zero* error (low extreme) or *overflow* (high extreme).

Test all sizes:

Another typical point of failure in custom and standard SAP processes would be volume. While creating a large volume of data to process may be troublesome and time consuming, it is a *necessary* part since technical coding can work and produce the right results when the input is small. However, they can *crater* when the volume gets large. Dreaded errors related to memory allocation, or technical ABAP limits can pop up. Runtime (not from a performance point of view) can also be an issue. No one wants slow running processes but if the process in question is executed online (i.e. not a batch job), there are generally limitations placed upon those processes to finish within a predetermined amount of time. Exceeding this time limit will generally result in a *system cancelled* process. This situation again would never reveal itself in testing if sufficient volume of input is not supplied to the test cases.

Test point in time:

While this type of testing does not reveal whether a process will crash or fail, it will illustrate potential *bad results*. Processes which are *"date sensitive"* may be impacted based on point in time. Not just calendar time but also business cycle period. Maybe a program expects to be executed *only* during the current accounting period. What if the program was executed *after* MEC? Will it still produce the *correct* results? What if the accounting period was reopened, will the program operate correctly? What about YEC (year-end close) whereby it is technically the *next* calendar year but still the *last* fiscal year? Another variation of this potential issue which requires testing would be *time zones*. For implementations which span multiple time zones, it is absolutely imperative that processes be sensitive to it. When dealing with custom programs / processes, it is best to either store time and date values in UTC[54] time zone or store the actual time zone along with the time and date. In short, one never wants to mix time zones in processing. Simple example: user is in CST, system is based on EST. Custom program stores the record creation time/date. User creates record at 11:30 PM CST. However, other processes store records in that table in system time (EST). So, when a query is performed, some records may be missed. Consistency is key. UTC is best. Storing the time zone is also an option. Using the user or system time zones is generally a bad idea due to potential issues.

Test communication:

Communication as in connectivity and interfaces to other systems (whether other SAP systems or third-party systems). This is often pushed to the bottom of the test list but should not be. Testing interfaces with systems which do NOT belong to your company generally becomes a logistic nightmare. Not only is getting a simple test case a difficult matter of coordination with the third party, repeating those tests may sometimes be very troublesome or impossible. The key to remember here is that having *no control* over third party's time, that should translate to having the *highest* probability to affect your project time line (i.e. high risk). Focus on this from the beginning and don't wait until the end. The *more* third parties are involved, the *higher* the risk.

Lather, rinse, repeat

Key with testing is repetition. In order for the stakeholders to feel comfortable with the risks associated with the project, multiple test cycles may need to be performed. With some processes (e.g. MEC), this becomes a logistic and data nightmare. So, what can be done to speed this up? If resources are available, one can employ a multi-system or multi-client strategy to speed things up. If the goal is to test MEC multiple times, do a backup *before* MEC. Test and reset. The fastest strategy is to have multiple systems (and costliest from a system resource point of view). Test one system. Reset it. While that system is being reset, testers can use the *second* system. If two systems are not available, one could use multiple clients within the same system to achieve the same. Test one client. Reset it. While that client is being reset, testers can use the second client. Two is not a limit. You could

---

[54] UTC is the primary standard by which the world regulates clocks and time. Previously used was Greenwich Mean Time (GMT). UTC does not have daylight savings changes, so in effect it never changes, thus why it's called universal. In SAP UTC is typically stored in year, month, day, hours, minute and seconds. For example, November 20, 2021 at 10:00AM and 0 zeconds would be stored as **20211120100000**

use five systems/clients (or as many as resources allow) to minimize wait time for system reset. Multiple systems are faster because a *system restore* is the *quickest* method to reset versus a *client reset* would in essence be a *client import* which is generally slower. Also keep in mind the coordination of third party test systems. When you reset your system, they may have to do the same or worse, they may not be able to. Your testing must keep this in mind.

Chapter V – Data Conversion

"An information system only has value when people use it correctly." Stephen Harwood.

Criticality of Data Conversion

Data conversion is an *often-overlooked* area that can cause significant issues for an SAP Finance implementation. Since most financial system implementations are planned for go-live January 1st, and since the actual data or books need to be *financially closed* in the prior system, this is very often an area with many challenges. Just because the last transactional data will not be available to upload sometime after the last *December month-end close* in the prior system, does not mean you cannot plan and test data conversion several months beforehand. The earlier you *plan* and *test* data conversion processes, the smoother it will go during implementation.

Chart of Accounts Considerations

There are several questions to consider whenever a client is implementing SAP S/4 HANA Finance. Following are sample questions:

- Is the client implementing a *brand new* general ledger account numbering system? If they are, how are they planning to go from their *prior* GL account numbering system to the *new one* in SAP? Please note that all possible combinations are challenging (i.e. going from *fewer accounts* to *more* GL accounts in SAP or vice-versa). The key is to have a translation or cross reference of the *old* to the *new* elements early on. As discussed further not only will GL account balances have to be taken into consideration, but also additional elements like functional areas, profit center, cost centers, transaction types, trading partners, vendors, customers etc....

- Are they retaining their *prior general ledger* account numbering system? This area may need to potentially be evaluated *further* since as discussed on chapter III, to take advantage of SAP's full reporting functionality with additional elements (like cost center category, functional area, trading partner and many others) *most non-SAP* general ledger account numbering systems do not take these elements into consideration. In other words, most GL account numbering systems are "flat" in the sense that almost every *attribute* about an *expense* or *revenue* transaction is contained in the GL account number itself. Having to rely on a legacy GL account numbering system would require several additional attributes, which increases transaction processing complexity.

- How will the data conversion process be loaded in SAP? Will it be a *big bang* approach or *sprinkled* throughout the project? In general, a big bang approach is not the recommended course of action as certain data, particularly master data, could be loaded in the system sooner than after December close. The sooner data is loaded into the development and acceptance systems, the better it will be for the project. Even using *test data* from the prior fiscal year from the prior financial system would be beneficial, since it will give a chance to project stakeholders to get familiar with many aspects and avoid potential errors.

- How are you planning to address master data conversion vs. transactional data (i.e. balances) to be loaded in the new SAP system? Are you planning on retaining any numbering system for master data from the prior system or are you starting with a *brand-new* numbering system?

- How many years of experience in the *actual business process* does the team or teams handling data conversion have? The higher the years of experience, the easier it will be to understand the different implications and nuances of accounting data conversion. For example, data conversion for GL accounts is simpler than say for conversion of *Tax-only* fixed assets in the Fixed Assets module since a lot more attributes need to be taken into consideration.

Starting with a brand-new SAP GL account numbering system

SAP comes default with a *pre-configured* GL account master data already being created as part of SAP's "Model Company" approach, which is typically pre-configured by industry[55] type. This model company setup would generally include most commonly used GL accounts by the different industries. One of the challenges with this setup, although good to start for a company migrating from a non-SAP system, is that by necessity additional GL accounts would need to be created. There are several potential reasons why additional GL accounts may need to be created:

- Accounting policy interpretations would vary company to company. Even though two companies would be in the same industry and use the same accounting principles (e.g. U.S. GAAP), they would still

---

[55] https://www.sap.com/services/implementation/preconfigured-industry-solutions.html

have differences in accounting staff, different management requirements and styles. Some companies like to have a *very low level* of detail in their GL account numbering systems, while other companies like to leverage additional attributes in the SAP world to provide reporting needs. In general, it is best to rely more heavily on additional SAP attributes (i.e. material number/group) to provide a *more robust* financial reporting and *minimize* GL account maintenance for *redundant* accounts.

- Bank account setups would be different, with some companies having multiple bank accounts in multiple *foreign currencies*, while another company having only USD bank accounts with a few banks.

- Compensation plans and bonus structures. For example, a company may have detailed bonus or incentive plans that it would like to categorize in different GL accounts for financial reporting purposes.

- Different management and internal reporting structures that would need to be factored in the GL account setup. Although it is best to rely on segment, business area or company codes to provide this level of reporting, by necessity some GL accounts might need to be created to differentiate *between* product sales and pipeline fees.

Early review of Data conversion

Conducting *early reviews* of the financial data to be converted can increase the changes of a project having reliable financial data to report on for the next fiscal year. It is not recommended to *wait* until the *last minute* (i.e. after December has closed for the prior year on the prior system) to start reviewing data conversion requirements and details. The earlier the better. It is also a good practice to start having *incremental* and *frequent* mock data conversion loads along the way and could be argued that it should be one of the first tasks undertaken in a system conversion, even prior to having some of the first IT or User tests available. Most system upgrades struggle significantly with having relevant and applicable data scenarios and a well-defined data conversion could provide the much-needed scenarios needed to test out the many new functionalities and customizations being built in the new SAP S/4 HANA system.

Considerations for Data Conversion

When analyzing the different sets of both *master* and *transactional* data, it becomes quite imperative to a have detailed plan and list of requirements for the different types of data and periods. Sample questions to think about:

- What are the detail characteristics needed not only at the *balance level* but also for each individual transaction? For example, for open item transactions, each individual transaction since inception needs to be kept, what are the elements need to further down the road clear these transactions? Will those be posted correctly in the conversion load? What is the strategy on aging of these open items?

- Is there a required comparison period that is needed in the new system? For example, typically, most financial accounting and reporting requirements compare prior month to current month, prior quarter to current quarter, prior year quarter to this this year quarter and year-to-date comparison for the prior year vs. current year.

- Are there other sub-ledger or other modules to think about in terms of loading data conversions? For example, logistics such as sales & distribution, materials management, plant maintenance or industry specific modules such as Production Revenue Accounting? These data modules will need to have a separate data conversion since for legal or tax reasons they may need to have a longer retention period. For example, for data conversion of factory equipment, for warranty purposes, there might be a requirement to keep the last 5 or 7 years' worth of maintenance history. Although not covered by this book, it is a good idea to engage other teams beyond your SAP finance team to gain a perspective on how they will be accomplishing data conversion. There could be potential tools or processes that could be shared among the different IT teams.

- Are the different teams in the different Finance and Non-Finance groups talking to each other frequently and sharing common integration points? For example, for team a field could be irrelevant for their process but for another team it could be mean the difference between a catastrophe and a successful execution of data conversion (i.e. trading partner or fixed assets level of detail). Be sure to schedule frequent "touch points" along your SAP project implementation to keep a hold of how

- Start thinking and planning for a potential *mock-up* balance load in the development and acceptance environments. Starting early in the project can lead to many benefits, the earlier the better. Do not wait until the last month once the books are closed in the prior system to do true system loads into SAP. What may look like a low risk or easy transition into SAP, could have multiple levels of complexity due to validations, missing data fields and incorrect configuration.

- Data should be loaded, to the extent feasible, at the *lowest level* of detail available. Remember it's easy to sum or aggregate records, but almost next to impossible to subtract records in different levels of detail (i.e. a program can sum-up the total activity for different cost centers to come up to a total at the company code level, but if data is posted to only 1 cost center, it is almost next to impossible to reverse engineer the detail).

- Is the data conversion team well-versed in both SAP and the prior system? At least a couple of the team members should be well-versed in the old system and be able to effectively translate the *meaning* and *intent* of a particular data field.

- Do you have updated, accurate and up to date well-defined definitions of *every* single element to be loaded into the new system? It is critical to have both the definition and the intent of a particular master or transactional data element. This should help alleviate disagreements down the road since all the stakeholders will be aware and hopefully be on board with the data conversion.

Balance Sheet vs. Income Statement

In general terms, the least complex financial data conversion is to usually bring in the *ending* balances from the prior system, which will then will become the *beginning* balances in the new SAP system. In addition to initial balances, many financial and regulatory reports typically require a 3-yr comparison period, particularly for income statement and balance sheet. Many other jurisdictions or areas might even require an *inception-to-date* comparison or running total, which increases the complexity of the data conversion process.

The other challenge is that typically income statement accounts' activities *prior to the original* go-live should not technically be loaded in SAP, since they close out to retained earnings in the income statement. For some of these reports requiring historical income statement data, you may need to consider custom tables that would be loaded for prior year activities *before* the initial go-live in January. This approach has an enormous advantage during IT and user testing, since users can run comparison reports and understand trends in the prior data and allow the project to *clone and re-post* historical data in the development or acceptance environment in SAP. Another approach would be to consider some sort of data warehouse solution that houses the summarized or *as-reported* data from the prior financial system and harmonizes it with the newly created reports/statements from the new SAP system. Both approaches are valid and depends on the level of detail that the customers will need to have in the source SAP system.

Open Item Migration

In SAP balance sheet accounts can be setup as balance forward, open item, vendor/customer of asset accounts. For open item GL accounts, not only the ending balance of the prior system needs to be loaded, but also the underlying activity that comprises or justifies that balance. In addition, for account reconciliation purposes, in many organizations, open items need to be aged based on different criteria, therefore it is important to retain these original postings in the data conversion. For example, for some documents in SAP using the *document date* is appropriate, for some other documents using the *posting date* for account aging purposes is acceptable. No matter the requirements or the fields, these document line items need to retain those original elements from the prior system in order to be successfully aged and reported. If the underlying detail is not preserved, accounts risk to be incorrectly aged and reported, losing historical information and potentially exposing the financial function for an audit finding. Otherwise, for example, all transactions, even if they were posted in the original system 5-yrs ago and are still open, risk being "reset" and have the new age based on the *data conversion posting date*, which will be incorrect.

Customer and Vendor Master Data

Customer and Vendor master data is among the most critical elements of a well-executed SAP project and one of the often most *overlooked* areas. Throughout the web, we can find many instances of incorrect customer or vendor setups leading to *wrong* or *double payments*, angry customers or vendors, loss of reputation, impacts to cash flow and collections and many other horror stories. Data *privacy* is another key component in this space, since both of these areas interact with highly confidential data such as social security or tax ID numbers, bank account numbers, addresses and much more. Having a robust customer and vendor master data conversion is very critical for a successful implementation. The other additional complexity in this space is the fact that interfaces will generally have to play a key role. A good example of how interfaces can impact end-customer or vendor relationships are with the customer or vendor number. In the old legacy system, the customer or vendor account numbers were probably different than the newly assigned numbers in the new SAP system, so having that cross reference of old master data to new master data numbers should be one a key deliverable of the project. Another area to think about is on the *numbering logic* for customers and vendors, in other words, is the numbering logic simple to understand (i.e. use customers starting with 9 for internal customers, 8 for international, etc…). Also, does the numbering logic allow for *growth* in the business? One of the worst decisions that can happen is that the implementation *runs out* of customer and vendor numbers.

For example, for U.S. Tax, 1099 forms reporting is an IRS requirement, and typically third-party vendors provide these services, so having an early engagement with these providers, months or 1 year before go-live becomes a necessity. The other additional consideration in this space is Business Partners or BP (in S/4, BP numbers are used for customer and vendor and many other relationships), is the mass creation of BP[56]. Lastly, but not least, since this is a very sensitive area, the security testing and SAP roles design for BP can be one of the most challenges aspects of a project (for example, who should have access to update a bank account in a vendor number, etc.…). Having a good design with all these considerations planned out in advance is quite important overall.

Customer and Vendor Balances and Activity

Similar to GL account open items, but with far more impactful external consequences, including legal exposure, are the data conversion process for customer and vendor *balances and activity*. As discussed in the master data section, particularly for customers, being able to access their historical data in the prior format is critical. For example, a customer may have built an entire reporting system based on a particular CSV or Excel based report and not being able to provide to the customer in the same format, frequency or data quality could lead to loss of business, particularly in highly competitive industries such as fuel marketing or commodities in general. Additionally, many credit departments would need to have historical and detailed customer transaction activity, so it will be important to understand early on *how* and *where* this additional customer activity will be stored beyond the initial data conversion of customer/vendor activity in SAP FI. Lastly, and related to system go-live, the communication and interface update with external parties is also critical for cutover processes. For example, having well defined procedures for areas such as payments made or received during cut-over activity is highly recommended to avoid having duplicate records (old system

---

[56] As of the time of this writing, there's no mass creation standard SAP solution for Business Partners

and new SAP installation). In addition, implementing good management of change practices with customers and vendors and potentially staff up representatives to handle the anticipated number of calls to the vendor or customer system should be a priority. The more prepared your customers and vendors are to the upcoming transition the better it will be for all parties involved.

Project Financial and Fixed Assets Records

Fixed assets in another area where having a well-defined data conversion plan cannot only make go-live more manageable but also the first *year-end close* in the new system. It is also important to understand how the prior financial system kept asset records, and how the prior systems' chart of accounts was setup. Did the prior chart of accounts define types of expenses? (i.e. GL account X defined whether a particular expenditure was capital or expense) as this would drive additional considerations of data elements in SAP. For project financial postings, there will need to be additional considerations for the different stages of project (assets under construction conversion for example).

Below are a couple of potential questions to brainstorming your asset records data conversion strategy:

- Will the project be closed out *before* the system goes live and will already be a fixed asset in depreciation?
- What would be the projects, both expense and capital, that would *still be in flight* during the go-live of the new SAP systems? For those, the original transactions since project inception would have to be migrated and posted to created WBS elements and rolled up into project definitions and a cut-over will have to be put in place for new transactions to start originating in the new SAP system and no longer be routed in the old financial system. For example, if you retain the same numbering scheme for WBS elements from the prior system, potentially this would lead to less short-term disruptions at the *cost of flexibility and full functionality* of the system. A new numbering scheme would take potentially advantage of being able to catalog the different types of WBS elements in the naming or numbering convention (i.e. WBS element prefix CAP for capital projects, etc..)
- Do you need to load *historical project data* for projects that have been closed out and already depreciated in the old financial system? Some organizations like to keep historical project data to do returns or efficiency calculations for looks back and that sort of thing. Some of

the needs may need to be addressed through a data warehouse solution instead of relying on SAP PS system.

In the fixed assets side, depending on the number of *depreciation areas*[57] that you will need, the quality of asset data quality could vary substantially. In some conversions, only the main financial asset records are maintained up to date, with assets for non-financial depreciation areas, such as Tax, are not kept in sync, leading to inconsistencies in the reporting (i.e. an asset would have been retired a long time for financial purposes, but still keeps depreciating for tax purposes, leading to a gap). Some of these challenges would have to be taken into consideration not only for data conversion purposes for but also for *fixed assets configuration purposes*. The general guidance for fixed assets is to try to setup the different depreciation areas as *flexible* as possible in terms of *accounting principle*[58], that way corrections can be made for the non-financial depreciation areas without impacting the main financial depreciation area.

Other considerations for fixed assets:

- Is the level of accounting detail for the other depreciation areas the same as the financial side? Does one depreciation area require a much more detailed level of accounting that the main depreciation area? How significant or critical is this depreciation area?

- Depending on the number of assets, it might be more appropriate to setup assets specifically for that depreciation area (for example tax-only assets).

- How well kept is the prior financial system asset records? When was the last time that a *physical to book* reconciliation was performed? One of the outcomes that could happen is that as a result of the migration to SAP, many data conversion issues could be found that would be *unnecessarily blamed* on the system instead of having *bad initial data quality* in the first place. This is why starting earlier in the data conversion process, even with less than *current data* from the prior system, is ideal, as it would allow your team to asks these types of

---

[57] Depreciation areas are used in SAP to calculate parallel or different values for different reporting needs. For example, you could have a depreciation area for external reporting (associated with accounting principle U.S. GAAP) and one depreciation area for internal reporting. Another example would be to have several tax related depreciation areas in the same Income Tax accounting principle (i.e. State Income Tax, Federal Income Tax, and so forth).

[58] Accounting principle allows a company to have multiple valuation approaches. All implementations must have a *leading* accounting principle (for example U.S. GAAP). Additional accounting principles can be setup to satisfy needs for U.S. Income tax compliance, IFRS, local GAAP, etc…

questions and play with the data. As the old adage says *"Garbage in, garbage out"*. Recent incidents with data conversion including having converted an asset that was retired 20 years ago and it was still being depreciated in the prior financial system.

- Is there a single group or multiple groups that maintain the integrity of the asset data in the old financial system? Typically, if more than one group is involved, be assured that there will be communication issues among those different groups and potentially different requirements and data quality levels. Having early engagement and buy-in from the multiple stakeholder groups in the fixed assets area would be important. Remember that for one group may be the most critical data element, for another group it might be more of a cursory or irrelevant field.

- For the non-financial posting depreciation areas (i.e. those areas not posting in S/4 Asset Accounting to ACDOCA or the Universal Journal), be aware that SAP data model in this space is continuously evolving[59], some additional quality assurance on the evolution in the data model might be warranted.

Other Sub-Ledger records and Non-Financial Data

So far, we have covered some of major areas in Financials, but there are many other areas to consider, among few to mention:

- In the oil & gas industry in particular, the inclusion of Joint Venture Accounting (JVA) and Production Revenue Accounting require their own dedicated financial data conversion teams due to the extensiveness of business requirements, complex and evolving data model and multiple sub-ledger functionality. In addition, both models rely heavily on Business Partner functionality in S/4 now, so it is critical to have a detailed plan and very experienced personnel in this area in order to have a successful data conversion.

- Logistics, such as Materials Management and Sales & Distribution, have special requirements as well. If your implementation includes MM and SD functionality, for sure having a specialized data conversion team to handle the complex requirements of these two modules is a necessity. These modules have extensive capabilities and business process requirements beyond a financials

---

[59] As of the time of this writing in March 2021, for example the system is unable to calculate gain/loss in certain newer reports in Fiori for non-financial depreciation areas. Be sure to test out the non-financial or statistical posting depreciation areas in your implementation.

implementation and at the same time are tightly integrated with financial data. For example, CO-PA or Profitability Analysis is heavily reliant on the data coming from MM/SD, so it is quite important to establish shared objectives between the financial data conversion teams and the logistics teams. If you have a CO-PA implementation in your Finance SAP team, be sure to work very closely with the MM/SD teams.

Inclusion into User Testing

Having this conversion data available early on for IT and User testing will significantly simplify the time and effort spent on the IT team on creating scenarios for testing. Having a large, largely complete set of data to perform both unit and integrated tests can allow the project team to detect errors early on and make corrections to programs, business processes and much more. In addition, the availability of this testing will significantly make the actual testing go much smoother since users will have some data they can relate back from their original system. Lastly, the user testing will be a lot more meaningful since calculations with real data will be validated instead of dummy data being created.

Technical Point of View

Data conversion is one of those parts of most projects whereby a firm set of standards and rules will be beneficial. While it may restrict design freedom, having technical guidelines for all conversion programs to follow is a must.

Data Central

The first guideline is to *centralize the conversion* effort where the actual legacy value is being converted to the new system value. Any type of mapping or translation should be done in this central repository. ALL conversion programs should rely on these common constructs and repositories. For example, create a centralized routine to convert legacy material numbers to new material numbers. Material number is used everywhere in the system. All converted data which involves material number should call this *same* function to convert legacy to new. If any type of change was to occur which affects the conversion, one would only have to update ONE program source to affect the entire project. Having each conversion program convert the material number takes time to code and maintain. Changes will have to be done in multiple places, thus taking time again. Worse, if some programs were missed, the material number in the new landscape will not be consistent. Having a central point of conversion will also allow for easier performance tuning. Various buffering strategies could be employed thus improving thru-put for all conversion programs.

Cross Reference

Within these centralized conversion routines, one should also implement an evergreen cross reference. In any typical implementation project, it is easy to think that once conversion is done, you will never need to go back and look at legacy versus new. This is however untrue in most cases. Chances are, there WILL be times when one realizes they need the legacy value or the translation between old and new. A cross reference table maintained by the central conversion routine would be ideal for such a use case. The storage cost is minimal at best compared to needing it in the future and not having it. There are some SAP master data tables which hold legacy values. Make use of these when possible to minimize custom development[60].

What's in a Name?

Covered earlier in the book, the usage of smart numbering or naming conventions can be useful. If your legacy master data did not have it, now is your chance. Besides naming of new master data in the SAP landscape, another "name" is very important – the user name. Specifically, the user name used for conversion. Reason this is emphasized is that without a doubt, the conversion activity will be repetitive before go-live. Whether it is to validate translation, run mapping rules or mock up how long cut-over will take – the conversion step may likely be executed multiple times. While a system refresh to allow subsequent conversion runs is ideal, it often can take a long time. While one would never advocate direct table updates, if your project / team will employ such a method – being able to identify the converted data (i.e. created or changed by a special conversion user name) would be a major boon. Even if no repetition of the conversion will occur, having a special user name associated with the creator of specific data provides valuable information if any errors were to arise in the future. If the data was created by the special user – one knows where to start looking (i.e. conversion routines).

Timing is Everything

Even in the simple case of master data, there can be cascading conversions. What is meant by cascading conversions? When a piece of converted data is dependent on another piece of converted data, that is sometimes referred to as cascading conversion. One simple example could be bill of materials. One

---

[60] For example, you can rely on appending fields to cost center table CSKS or WBS element table PRPS.

cannot convert a BOM until the constituent materials have been converted. So, these conversions can only be done in *serial* and not *parallel*. The project needs to lay out all these data conversion activities to see which must be done in sequence and which can be done simultaneously. Another aspect of time is performance. Performance of conversion programs become a factor as more serial conversion appear in the project scope. If possible, static (or very infrequently changed legacy master data) should be moved *ahead of schedule* and a mini conversion go-live may be considered. This way, less are in the critical path during the mass go-live. Time comes into play again when we deal with non-master data. Open items, balances, etc. are time sensitive. Unless the legacy system has been shut down and no more transactions are posted, the cut-over period is very time sensitive. Related data must be converted "together". For example, when open items are migrated, the balance must reflect those items. If those two pieces of information are handled by two different conversion processes, there can be NO changes to the open items when the balances are migrated (and vice versa). So quiet time is a must. And quiet time generally means no business is conducted (in the legacy system) during the conversion process. In a utopian world, everyone would get out of the legacy system. The conversion team would work their technical magic. The new system is flipped on and all users start conducting business in the new system and never look back. However, in the real world, that is often not the case. Based on the amount of data which needs to be converted and the performance of the conversion programs, the cut-over period may be too long for the business not to transact in some system (legacy or new). In such a case, very careful planning is required to create a staged conversion / migration. The ultimate pool of data which needs to be migrated is critically analyzed and split into logical chunks whereby thus allowing the conversion to occur in phases. This way, business can continue. This is of course not without risk but often is something which cannot be avoided.

The Gift that Keeps on Giving

While everyone wishes for a one-time conversion and move to the new system, the reality is that often times, the legacy system needs to continue to exist AND used. In this case, what started as a conversion morphs into an interface which may live on for a long time. The guidelines used during the conversion should be followed to ease this pain point. In general, all those gotchas continue to exist in an ongoing legacy interface.

Chapter VI – Feedback Mechanism

"The impact of the human factor on the degree and effectiveness of ERP assimilation supersedes the technological factors." Kouki, Pellerin

What is a feedback mechanism?

A feedback mechanism, as the name implies, is the different ways to obtain feedback in any project, but as it applies in this book, particularly in software development and in SAP.

In other words, how would you know what you are developing in SAP or configuring in customization fits the *customer needs?* This question goes beyond the traditional testing cycles with the different phases of IT/unit testing, user testing and beyond. Establishing a sound feedback mechanism of continuous input that flows with the *minimum of gate keepers* to avoid the *telephone* problem or translation issues is vital to ensure expectations are largely met when the project goes live. There are several ways to establish a good feedback mechanism not just centered around end-user testing but all along the way, from *idea* to *development* to *deployment* to *production.*

Early Prototyping

Early prototyping is one technique to mitigate some risks in your project. Having users receive that early feedback is priceless. Early prototyping can provide many advantages, such as:

- Identify early SAP ABAP code issues, such as performance, amount of data processing and other technical concerns.

- Identify and map out data relationships in SAP (i.e. this table should have this field created as a primary key vs non-key) or should this field be stored as *rows* instead of *columns?*

- Help key users visualize how design elements like the selection screen, ALV output and required fields should be developed. This will minimize potential development recycles in the future, helping improve the final product.

- Helps get *buy-in* from the end-customer along the way of the development of the program since they were involved early-on to provide constructive feedback. In other words, they would be more involved since they "own" the development in a way.

- Prototyping can substantially reduce the probability of *pie-in-the-face* type of scenarios whereby user requirements were not conveyed successfully to the IT team and the final product is a disaster.

- Identify potential gaps in the data being analyzed or processed by the program. For example, are cost center categories consistently used in all cost center master data creation processes?

Full end-to-end data

As master and transactional data moves through several financial processes, it might potentially lose elements or be incorrectly derived. Examples include:

- Having an incorrect profit center being derived on a SD module sales order.

- Allocations not being setup correctly and allocating the wrong cost elements to cost centers. So, for example, even though first incurred costs might have been recorded correctly in FI-GL, by the time allocations are run, several key components may not be correctly derived (for example vendor information not being recorded on expenditure accounts).

- Taxation items, such as tax jurisdiction code, input tax parameters and many others.

- Trading partner, critical for intercompany eliminations of sales and expense transactions.

- Subledger to general ledger elements may not be available. Examples include fixed assets data, production revenue accounting, CO-PA, MM or SD elements.

This transformation and derivation of data has to be analyzed separately. A good idea might be to map out how the different data elements flow through the system, from creation or change, to initial posting, subsequent allocations/reposting all the way through reporting. In addition, many times, one element depends on another element (example of tax jurisdiction code being derived from the cost center the entry is posted to), so that needs to be considered as well.

Importance of aligning with key stakeholders

Throughout the month-end close, in most large and medium companies, there are different key stakeholders in the Finance or Controllers groups. Example of groups that a typical company would have in their different functions in a Controllers organization:

- Financial Accounting
- Financial Reporting
- General Accounting
- Revenue Accounting
- Internal Controls & Internal Audit
- Cost accounting
- Projects & Fixed Assets Accounting

Another factor that comes into play is the fact that many of these groups would have a different use case for SAP Finance or potentially may not even use SAP at all or rely on a third-party solution for their specific needs. This is important to note since it impacts their view on how *critical* or *needed* an SAP process might be.

The other challenge involved in an SAP implementation, particularly those that are greenfield or switching from a non-SAP system, is that the same subject matter experts in those different finance or controller's groups might be overwhelmed with day-to-day activities and requests. As the phrase goes *"if you want something done, give it to a busy person"* rings true in these implementations more than ever. Being able to effectively use these highly sought-after SME's time in an SAP implementation will be critical. It is essential other accounting SME's gain knowledge in parallel and assist in the discovery process so that the more advanced SME can weigh on decisions and not have their valuable time misused in answering basic questions when in discovery mode.

Availability of transaction or programs to key power users

It may sound obvious, but many times access or security could be a constrain to power users. Power users and users with curiosity and a knack for problem solving, should be granted additional access (even beyond what their role would typically call for) in a sandbox, prototype or even acceptance environment since they will help find solutions, identify problems early on to avoid costly mistakes. In addition, they could potentially find new transaction codes to use or new processes that could create additional benefits to the SAP project. Harnessing these key users' curiosity is an asset for any SAP project.

Identifying dependencies early on

The earlier dependencies can be identified the better it will be for the project implementation. Following are some potential ways to identify these dependencies early on:

- Start with the *very end of the process* in mind. Early on in your discovery and design alignment phase of your project, meet with the *ultimate recipients* of financial data of your system. These could be personnel in the financial reporting groups or even further *upstream* of that, like business unit personnel or managers. Document & understand what some of the key values and metrics that they use to analyze the performance of their business. What are they focusing on?

- There could be multiple end-user stakeholder groups with different requirements for financial data. For example, the group in charge of financial statements & consolidation of financial results will be very dependent on reliability of say *trading partner data*, while for a field business unit analyst the trading partner might be less of a concern with opex reporting being more critical. Keep these differences in mind when engaging the different teams, one "irrelevant" piece of data for one team could be another team's much needed "treasure".

- All levels in your project team should be somewhat aware of key reports and ultimate financial deliverables. A key few members in your project team should get up to speed quite fast with the ultimate financial reports or deliverables with the goal of becoming SMEs. For example, how does the organization evaluate financial performance at the lowest level in the organization could be quite different how the external reporting team handles financial statement at the corporation level, segment or company code level. Understand these differences and needed SAP data elements to produce these set of reports. In addition, it might be good to attempt to try rank these data elements in order of importance of not having an *available workaround*. For example, not having one field that could be derived from another field would be less of a concern if another field has to be captured at the time of posting (for example document date, which has to be entered as part of financial posting vs. tax jurisdiction which hypothetically could be derived *after-the-fact* from cost center master data).

- Provide regular updates, whether through email or through a scorecard, of the progression of identifying and confirming and understanding of those dependencies. Increasing the visibility of those dependencies along the way will make lives easier for everybody involved as well as avoid statements like "we were not aware this field was used by this group" 2 years down the road.

- Having a full simulated month-end or quarter close, even with sample data, will give a preview of some of the dependencies to understand and tackle. For example, with basic test data, could you run a full set of financial statements and have it as a preview to the financial reporting team? If so, this might help mitigate some unknowns as you progress in your SAP Finance implementation.

Technical Point of View

Prototyping is a powerful approach as a feedback mechanism during the implementation. However, as all good ideas, one must take note of the potential pitfalls so at the end, the cons do not outweigh the pros.

Litter Bug

Not bug in the traditional program bug but litter bug as in the proliferation of dead, obsolete, useless development objects. During the prototyping process, many objects will be created (programs, screens, functions, tables, etc.) One of the major benefits of prototyping is "trying out" an idea. Whether it is to mock up a screen or test out proposed business logic implementation, these objects may be transient. At the end of that specific prototype, those objects may not be necessary. The maintenance / management of development objects is highly dependent on the number and complexity of said objects. Cleaning up "garbage" objects will dramatically decrease the overall maintenance effort post go-live. So, the rule of thumb would be to delete all unused prototype objects as soon as they are no longer needed. Trying to ascertain the justification for an object during a long project may be difficult if the objects are kept until the end of the project.

Organization

There are several different ways to stay organized and help keep litter to a minimum. If all the required data needed to test are present in the development system, then creating prototype objects as *"local objects"* is one approach. These local objects can never leave the development system as they are. If the data needed to test out a prototype is only available in an acceptance system, then these objects must be assigned to a development package and transported. Recommendation here would be to create a new development package just for prototyping and assign all prototype created objects in this new package. This way, there is an easy way to discover what the purpose of an object would be. If the prototype is successful and the decision is made to keep the prototype and go live with it, simply reassign the associated objects from the prototype development package to the actual target development package. If those objects are not needed, they should be deleted in the development system, released, and ultimately imported as it would yield a *net change of zero.*

Streamline

Keeping the development objects to a minimum pays large dividends post go-live in several ways. Time of technical impact analysis is greatly reduced (i.e. if a change is made to this object, what other processes or objects will it impact). When upgrade time rolls around, the potential remediation effort would be reduced.   Total cost of ownership is reduced since any issues found will more likely be an issue within the standard SAP functionality (and thus would have SAP support).

Chapter VII – Code Quality & Importance of ABAP

"No company, no manager is sufficiently brilliant to think about all of the complexities and complications inherent in a cross-functional ERP project." Thomas Davenport.

Background on ABAP

ABAP stands for Advanced Business Application Programming language and has been in use by SAP since the 1980's in SAP's R/2 version. Developed by SAP specifically for SAP, ABAP was the only programming language of choice for many SAP releases. With the move to the internet, Java was later introduced as an alternative but ABAP remains the main language used in the development of the ERP software.

Procedural Programming

ABAP being based off of COBOL and PL/1 started off as purely procedural. Procedural programming language like its name suggests is basically a programming language which runs procedures. *Line by line*, code is executed in a linear fashion. Understanding this type of coding is relatively simple. Various language constructs were introduced to allow for some level of code reuse or maintenance consolidation. Functions being the biggest reuse components within ABAP, it's also the foundation and forefather of web services.

Object Oriented Programming

As the software industry matured, the concept of separating the "display" or "visualization" of the program from the business logic became more prevalent. A popular programming paradigm known as MVC (model, view, controller) lead SAP to enhance the procedure programming language of ABAP to be slightly object oriented. By no means a pure object-oriented programming language, ABAP now does have various OO constructs to allow for encapsulation, inheritance, and basic forms of polymorphism via interfaces. These OO features of ABAP also formed the basis of SAP's web initiative since the rendering of the user interface is generally done by the web browser and having an adaptive display like a tablet or mobile phone. However, please take caution in that just because the object oriented (and MVC) paradigm are newer and more advanced than procedural programming methods, different situations may call for a different methodology. Object oriented programming shines when *inheritance* is heavily used. The ability to redefine a portion of a large chunk of programming or code is a major boon.

However, the usage of object-oriented programming can come at a price. With talk of DevOps these days, the concept of technical debris or useless artifacts come into the picture. One single procedural program may be sufficient for a task while developing it using OO may involve multiple objects. The total cost of ownership of multiple technical artifacts could outweigh the benefits of the new methodology. There is no one best method.

ABAP Developer Experience and Expertise

The term "developer" is loosely used these days. Generally, it is defined as personnel within the information technology department who knows a specific programming syntax and can utilize that knowledge to write programs for a specific business need. Learning the syntax of a language is trivial. Anyone with time and a basic understanding of programming can pick up a new language and utilize the tools involved to write programs. But can anyone actual develop *good software*? Is an ABAP programmer any different than programmers of other languages? The short answer is yes. Reason is because ABAP was specifically designed to work within an SAP system. It does not operate anywhere else. Most other languages can be utilized in many other environments (Java, C, etc.) The main difference is that when it comes to ABAP, a thorough understanding of the *actual SAP system* makes a huge difference. Seasoned ABAP developers understand the landscape and how to best utilize it to create elegant software. It's not just code, it's actually a piece of the overall system.

Focus on performance

Any development effort which is to linger and utilized again periodically should be built with performance in mind. One time throw away programs "may" get a pass for the sake of *cost to benefit* ratio. While conversion programs (during cut-over) may be one time use development, they generally do not get this exemption because the cut-over time frame is often small and finite. Building common routines which can be called from various development can reduce maintenance but could also create bottlenecks if those common routines do not perform well. Performance scrutiny must be high especially in these common building blocks. Even a small bit of speed gain could sum up to huge reduction in overall runtime when that small bit of code is called repeatedly as often is the case. A balance needs to be achieved between speed and maintainability as the most efficient code may not always be the easiest to maintain or enhance.

New changes in S/4

While ABAP continues to evolve and improve with each NetWeaver release, the major advancement in S/4 HANA would be the database itself. The same ABAP coding techniques (without using newer ABAP features) can already be used to take advantage of HANA to obtain unbelievable speed gains if written properly. What HANA brings to the table turns the ABAP development mantras up on its head. For example, in the past the concept of adaptability was important. The usage of an ABAP construct to read every field from a database table (even if not all are used) can be preferred since doing so allows the program to continue working even if SAP was to add to or enhance the database table. However, in the HANA world, that is a major performance nightmare. Asking the database to retrieve all the columns (from a columnar database) is paramount to asking for the world especially when one does not need it. Any upgrades to HANA from ECC should at least involve a custom code evaluation. SAP offers some tools to analyze custom code to identify such issues. Make sure that is part of the project timeline.

CDS Views

Also known as core data services, CDS comes in two flavors – HANA and ABAP. Both are very similar. HANA CDS views are HANA artifacts which live inside HANA only whereby ABAP CDS views straddle the two. For all intents and purpose, they are the same type of construct. CDS views are mere representations of HANA data organized as "views". Annotations are made to augment these CDS views so various consuming engines can react differently. CDS views is the basis of all future SAP innovations. Fiori apps can often be built using nothing but CDS views and annotations with little to no traditional programming. CDS views are also built in layers to allow different consumers different ways of accessing the same data. Any SAP customer utilizing HANA should take note and invest in having a good CDS view strategy. Building custom CDS views haphazardly can yield disastrous results in both performance and maintainability.

Code Quality can make or break a system

Developing software to meet a business demand is easy. Maintaining said software is where the real cost comes into play. Code quality should be top priority with any SAP information technology department. Imagine if there is a production stop due to an error in some custom coding. If the program was developed in an organized fashion with high code quality, bug resolution or enhancement would be much simpler. On the contrary, if the object was developed with no regards for standards or maintainability in mind, the time to solve the issue could be much longer. As any business live by, time is money so putting effort into code quality from the onset will pay high dividends in the long run.

Horror Stories on bad ABAP programming

Taken from a real customer utilizing a custom developed process in S/4 HANA: the scenario involves fixed asset accounting. A specific business event required the company to transfer tens of thousands of assets (more specifically adjust their net book values). The custom process designed was to transfer all the needed assets to a transient asset and then transfer back from the transient asset to the original asset but with a different net book value. Doing so in essence would rebalance everything. Initial testing revealed no issues and even small usage cases yield no major problems. When the large scale real world scenario came, problem struck. This process (and thus programming) is linear in that it has to be all or nothing. Once an asset's value is transferred to the transient asset, the "total" within the company is the same but the original assets' value is reduced to zero during this rebalancing and won't get a value until the entire process completes. Unfortunately, performance degradation with large datasets came into play. The process was taking days. Days became weeks. During this entire time, there was no way to operate on these assets since the value was incorrect. Moreover, there was no way to reverse midway without taking the same amount of time again. In short, the customer was stuck. Having to not utilize the SAP system for those assets and capture everything on spreadsheets until said assets are freed back up and corrected in value. Post mortem analysis showed that from the beginning, the design was flawed. There was little to no re-startability. It had to complete or be unwound. A rethink and reprogramming of the process was needed. The revamped process now is more than 50x faster, can restart and recover any time, and always keep the asset values correct allowing them to eschew business quiet time for those assets.

Chapter VIII – To Customize vs. not to Customize

"Competitive advantage comes not from systems, but from doing something better than competitors." Thomas Davenport.

What is a customization?

It is important to start with a good definition of what constitutes a customization. A customization is any change to the way SAP operates that is beyond the defined options in SAP's control panel, SPRO. Building a new ABAP report that does not come "out of the box" from the SAP installation is a customization. Creating a user exit is a customization as well. Customization objects typically start with the letters Y or Z since SAP does not ship any standard program that starts with those letters.

Different Types of Customizations

Just like everything in life, the word customization entails different types. The following are different types of customizations and ranked in terms of complexity and requirement for design oversight:

1. Independent read-only report: these type of programs or reports pose *the least amount of impact* and risk to the system since they are not creating records or impacting any other processes' ability to post or create financial data. These type of custom reports or programs should be encouraged since they have the potential to automate businesses processes and discourage users from using spreadsheets. An example is a report that joins transactional data with several master data classifications, this report would allow end-users to *not* download data in Excel, create a bunch of vlookups and waste time massaging and converting data. For example, a report that calculates tax savings could help prioritize the work of finance employees to focus on a type of transaction to process first and could save millions of dollars. This type of report would almost be impossible to be achieved in Excel since Excel is limited to roughly less than 1million rows. Additionally, these types of reports have the added advantage of helping users more effectively visualize data in the system. Be open to these types of reports since they are usually low cost to develop and could save millions of dollars in preventing bad data. Lastly, avoiding users relying on Excel spreadsheet on financial reporting should always be encouraged as it minimizes overall risk to finance activities.

2. Custom programs that create records to custom tables only: these types of customizations are more complex than the read-only programs since they have more moving pieces. In particular, the ability to generate records requires a little bit more design and thought in place *before* developing. There is more complexity in developing these types of custom programs as well since the data model has to be carefully designed to ensure records are being generated to these custom tables appropriately. However, these customizations are less challenging than programs that post or create records in standard SAP tables since, *in general,* there's no risk of downstream dependencies. In case data is *incorrectly written* to these custom tables, the data could simply be *re-generated* or *re-created* in some cases by the custom programs. Lastly, in terms of performance, HANA does not bring the same incremental leap in performance in write operations, while in read situations like the custom read-only reports can truly shine with S/4.

3. User exits: user exits, as the name hints, are SAP defined customer allowed *customization points* that allow customer to add custom code to *inputs* and/or *outputs* of a particular *standard* SAP process. A good example of the usage of user exits are on general ledger validations or substitutions (t-codes GGB0 and GGB1). These user exit points allow the customer to build custom logic *before* a financial entry is posted and validate or substitute fields as needed. User exits, although very powerful, have to be very well designed and thought out before and truly tested. These user exits have the potential to stop users from doing financial postings or can substantially alter the quality of financial data. In addition, too many of these user exits can increase complexity substantially when upgrading to a newer version of S/4 HANA. In addition, these validations and substitutions could be conflicting among themselves, so they require careful design, end-to-end testing and need to involve all impacted stakeholders in the system, including subledgers or external interfaces posting into SAP Finance. The migration to a productive environment of these user exits is usually considered a high-risk change and should be migrated at a quiet time.

4. Custom programs that create records to SAP standard tables: These customizations, depending on the way they are coded, could be among the riskier custom implementations. For example, if a

custom program uses a standard SAP BAPI/BADI[61] to post to an existing table it is considered less risky since it is using the "connector" in a way to the standard SAP table and behaves more or less like a standard SAP program. In other hand, programs that write directly to SAP standard tables should be more closely reviewed since they could create inconsistent data causing other downstream processes to fail.

5. Enhancements: Enhancements are the most complex and challenging customizations in the SAP space. In general terms, they should be avoided since they bring significant stability issues to the SAP system and can potentially limit the ability of the customer to upgrade to newer versions of S/4 HANA. As to compare it to the world of automobiles, while a custom read-only program might be equated to plugging in an USB device in the car, an enhancement could be compared to changing the company provided fuel injectors for fully custom ones. They could work great, but if left unchecked they could cause unexpected damage to the engine all the way to not allowing the vehicle to operate to even create potential safety hazards. In addition, the level of testing required not just for initial implementation of the enhancement but subsequent upgrades should be estimated as to have a better idea of the true total cost of this enhancement. Many times, an enhancement might point out to a particular business process that should be re-thought or potentially challenged instead and not blindly followed and implemented in SAP.

Cost of Support of Customizations

The cost of support for customizations should be estimated and analyzed very carefully. Depending on the complexity of customization the support cost could be substantially lower or could be substantially higher.

Following are a couple of items to consider:

*   What type of customization is it? In general, total cost and long-run support costs of an enhancement are higher than the cost of support of a read-only report. A very complex and costly enhancement should point out in the direction of potentially having a different business process altogether than trying to replicate an older system business process in SAP. Enhancements should be justified with a

---

[61] BAPI - Business Application - commonly a function module that is normally RFC enabled as well and acts as a method of a business object.
A BADI is a Business Add-in - one of SAP's methods of implementing a user-exit or change to standard SAP code.

very detailed statement of benefits as well as have an estimate of the increased costs of testing and support of the existing SAP system. In general, the more "core" functionality an enhancement impacts, the higher the level of approval, detailed analysis and cost-benefit justification should have.

- What is the upgrade strategy of the customer? For a customer that plans to space out S/4 HANA upgrades to a couple of years instead of SAP's yearly cycle, some more complex customizations might make more sense in the short-term. The more complex the customization, potentially the higher level of integrated testing involved in an upgrade, so those should be factored in as well.

- What is the cost of base support if a report stops working vs. the SAP support fee? The reason to ask this question is that if a program continues to work, there is no inherent IT cost every year to maintain this functionality while for many SAP co-innovations or even to upgrade to a new S/4 HANA system there is a yearly support fee attached to that standard SAP product. In other words, whether the functionality work or does not work, the customer has to pay SAP a fixed fee. In contrast, for an internally developed customization by the IT department, costs are only incurred whenever the actual application stops working or needs to be improved, in other words, become more of a variable cost while the standard product might carry a steep fixed cost per year.

- How detailed or complex are your customizations? For example, do you have one development with hundreds of ABAP classes/methods and deep understanding of the ins and out of that development? Or do you have a collection of small independent reports or programs that can be more surgically fixed if there is an issue or something breaks? The higher the complexity and criticality of these customizations the more experienced the customers' in-house SAP developers should be.

Needed Customizations

Besides the classification of customizations from a *technical* perspective, it is also important to classify customizations in terms of *business value*.

In general terms, customizations that provide the customer with a *competitive advantage*, i.e. the customer by using custom code can outperform its competitors in different business criteria, should be pursued. By having a competitive advantage, a company might be able to enter new markets, increase shareholder value, increase automation and reduce operating costs, so these customizations provide a *high return on investment*.

The following lists are potential reasons why a customization might be needed:

- Competitive advantage, for example, say the development of a custom set of programs allows a company to create new products, new markets or increase revenues to the corporation. Assume SAP standard functionality does not cover a particular market, while SAP may deliver this functionality many years down the road, having a company wait until that functionality is availability is not a good business decision. For example, by entering a new market, a company might be able to increase net income by $200 million per year, a factor many times the cost of a potential customization. Typically, mostly customer-facing organizations like sales or marketing would have the ability to add such an increase to the bottom line. Other functions to consider are the different departments that handle tax, which could potentially have tax savings of millions of dollars.

- Transaction automation, for example, a custom program allows the customer to process 1,000 invoices in 1 hour versus having to use standard SAP process that would take to process the same number of invoices 2-3 days. This is a very valid reason to have this customization in place, which can potentially reduce millions of dollars of per year in cost to a company. In other words, by having automation, this company can stay or serve a market with very high transaction costs and capture that benefit.

- Cost reduction. A new customization allows to reduce full-time equivalent staff members in the Finance organization or free up their time to perform more value-adding work instead of having to work on spreadsheets. These types of customizations would typically have 60% return of investment of more types of returns and should be encouraged. Many times, organizations trying to save a couple of thousand dollars can end up spending millions of dollars in additional costs. Avoid being "penny-wise but pound foolish".

- Legal or tax requirements that cannot be accomplished with standard SAP software. Many times, a customization might be needed due to a legal requirement or tax compliance that SAP will not address as part of standard SAP software. These customizations should also be given the green light since they allow a company to stay in business and avoid large penalties and fines.

Weak examples of customizations that might not be needed:

- Inability to change an internal business process that does not provide a company a comparative advantage. Many times, a very unnecessarily complex customization should be re-thought as a business process problem instead of something to be solved by adding SAP custom code. If a business process is broken from the beginning, no matter how great solution might be, the process will remain broken.
- "Controls requirement", "It's required by audit". These statements should be carefully evaluated and documented, and not simply used as a way to not change business processes. Many best it is best to quote directly from the company's internal control standards and discuss with IT audit very closely to understand the ultimate *intent* of a control in place.
- "It's the way is always been done here". Another statement that should be carefully evaluated. Just because a process has been done for a long-time way does not necessarily mean that it should continue to remain the same. It is best to research the original intent of the report/control in place and work out what would meet that requirement instead of trying to replicate 100% of how the old system used to look.
- "We have always sent Manager X this report". For example, that manager may have received that report because the report was sent to the prior manager, but many not have any use or value for that particular report. If possible, it is best to meet directly with the ultimate recipients of a particular report to understand what they are ultimately trying to achieve, as many times intent can be lost in playing the "telephone game".
- "The prior manager liked to this see report this way". Same as before.

SAP Product Maturity and need for customizations

In general, the more *mature, established* and *widely* used SAP module is, the lower the need for customizations. The opposite is true with less mature and ever evolving modules of SAP. The older and more mature an SAP solution is, in general the lower the case for a customization should be made. In other words, that existing SAP solution has had the luxury of being tested by thousands of customers, so any request for a customization in an established mature SAP solution should be more highly scrutinized than a brand-new SAP product, with more potential functionality gaps.

For example, customizations in the General Ledger (GL) should have a harder case to make since the general ledger functionality in SAP, both before S/4 HANA and with S/4 HANA, has been around for decades and used by basically every single customer that uses SAP. On the opposite side, is SAP's TSW (Trader Suppliers Workbench), which is a supply & trading module of SAP. Even though it has been around since the early 2000's, this product is evolving still as the underlying business process (supply/trading) is also evolving, so customizations in this space make more sense than say GL.

The other point to make in this space is that functionality that may have existed in ECC or R/3 and is being reworked or transformed in S/4 HANA may require customizations as well. A good example of this is the Fixed Assets module in SAP, which also has been around for decades, but it is evolving and the data model is now changing with the move to the universal journal or ACDOCA. Even though the product or functionality might be mature, the data model is evolving causing potential for gaps in functionality.

Customizations that destabilize the system

There are several types of customizations that should be avoided, those that unnecessarily increase the complexity of the system when testing and those that make SAP upgrades significantly more complex. In addition, those customizations that are done purely because of a manager wants to see a report "this way" without any valid business reason should be avoided.

A couple of examples from prior implementations:

- Customizations that try to re-create long established SAP functionality. A good example is FI-GL document line item clearing. Trying to mimic the logic of clearing, which has evolved over many decades with the input from thousands of customers, is futile and a misuse of IT and Finance project team members' time. Customizations that try to clear line items outside SAP should be avoided.
- Document approval type of customizations. For example, trying to prevent a document from posting because in the prior system all manual journal entries were approved by supervisors created

unnecessary complexity in a business process that has worked very well for SAP for many years.

- Customizations to try to *"paper over"* underlying issues with poor master data. For example, trying to build custom cost center logic o try to retain a numbering scheme or to deal with errors in design from the past might not be the use of time and money.

- Customizations that require several degrees of manual confirmation by end-users, limiting the possibility of automating business processes down the road. For example, if a process requires the user to confirm the action 3-4 times before completing, this may prevent more automation to take place.

- Customizations that alter the "core" of SAP, for example customizations that do direct write to a core SAP standard table or customizations that impact core basis or database services.

The sometimes-irrational push for standardization

Along with many of the provided literature from SAP, there's always a push, sometimes a little bit irrational, to use "out of the box" software, which may not suitable for all business processes. Be careful with an "avoid customizations at all costs" type of philosophy since it might prevent to unlock value and increase the competitive advantage of an SAP implementation.

For example, say a customization might save the company $10M in taxes because of a better report, would you say no to that customization and wait for SAP to *potentially* come up with a report like that and leave $10M on the table? These types of questions are important to raise in an SAP project environment since the team might waste time and money trying to fit a standard SAP solution that may not work necessarily in that customer's case or an SAP functionality that simply is not ready for "prime time" in an implementation.

Source of competitive advantage

Good, well designed customizations can unleash massive competitive advantage over a customers' peers. In fact, having customizations that push the limit of the product and innovate are a great way for a customer to benefit from the solid foundation and structure of an SAP system while still maintain the ability of the system to adapt to ever changing needs and get solutions to market faster than SAP could design this new functionality.

For example, SAP may not decide to cater to the needs of a small market and develop new functionality or a module that may only be used by a handful of customers and not make economic sense for them to invest in. In addition, the great advantage of a strong in-house SAP IT team is the ability to quickly deliver a solution to meet business needs without having to wait for SAP to catch onto this new need. In fact, many of the features that SAP may have now standard can typically arise by SAP understanding how customers are customizing their already installed SAP systems.

SAP Programmer availability

Another consideration to have for SAP customizations is the degree and experience of SAP programmers in your SAP project.

A few questions to consider:

- How many years of experience do your SAP developers have? Are they fairly new or have they done multiple implementations in the same business process or module? For example, the data model on one module may be more complex in one module than in another.

- Do you have programmers on site where your functional analysts can communicate, particularly early on in the design process, and share ideas?

- Does your developer offer alternative solutions instead of blindly following design specifications? A good, talented and experienced SAP developer will typically suggest improvements in the design to improve customer experience or performance of the application.

- How experienced is the functional analyst providing the design specifications? A winning combination is to have a highly experienced and talented functional analyst paired with a very experienced ABAP developer. Typically, you may want to avoid having a less experienced functional analyst with a very inexperienced ABAP developer. If you have new functional analysts consider paired them with very experienced ABAP developers as it will improve the design specs on the functional analyst side and the ultimate quality of the finished product.

Short-term agility in customizations

Lastly, as previously discussed, customizations can provide a long-standing competitive advantage and can potentially allow a customer to have more agility. For example, independent read-only programs or reports are relatively fast to develop instead of a waiting for a *"big bang"* approach of an SAP provided solution. This could save time and money to customers that would like to move forward with SAP technology but do not want to wait for all bugs and quirks to be fixed by SAP beforehand. In other words, these quick customizations allow a customer to implement SAP and go with SAP standard functionality for the 80% of business processes and provide the remaining with custom functionality that can help bridge that gap.

Technical Point of View

It is a well-known fact that most SAP clients have some level of customizations in their SAP landscape. While SAP is truly flexible and presents best of breed functionality, the unique needs of any company may go beyond the options available out of the box. So, it is generally a foregone conclusion that some level of customizations is needed. Even when customers utilize SAP Cloud edition, some type of customization may be needed. SAP does have cloud offerings which do not permit any type of customizations but those are generally for new customers with limited use cases.   Most on-premise SAP installations will have some type of customization.

It's All in the Name – Again?

The term customization so far has been used to denote a deviation from the standard out of the box functionality. As previously denoted, there many forms of it.

- The technical term used for customizations found in the IMG would generally be referred to as "configuration". Most of what one can do in the IMG will not be wiped out during an upgrade. The client chooses to "configure" how the system should behave. To borrow the earlier analogy of a car, one could buy order a car with different engines, colors, interiors, etc. Those are all from the factory. The client merely picks what they want. Pick a hybrid engine? It'll have batteries included, etc. This type of configuration is generally kept during an upgrade unless the new version has circumvented that functionality completely or augmented that functionality which necessitate a configuration change.
- User exits (or Business Add-Ins) are SAP delivered points in the software whereby a client can alter the out of the box behavior via ABAP code. This is similar to following a recipe to make a cake. All the ingredients are mixed, etc. When it comes time to bake, the

standard baking instructions may say, "bake in standard oven for 30 minutes at 350 degrees". A "user exit" could be to replace the baking method with something else. Instead, the client can choose to bake the cake in convection oven for 20 minutes at 400 degrees. This type of deviation (while sanctioned) is considered use at your own risk. There is no way for SAP to know how you will bake the cake. So, the steps after may or may not fit. The original recipe could say, let it rest for 15 minutes before icing. With the new method used via the user exit, the cake could be too warm still after 15 minutes. Icing the cake then could cause the icing to melt. This is a prime example of having to understand fully what the ramifications are while using a user exit.

- Next in line would be enhancements. Enhancements are newer than user exits in that it comes in both explicit (similar to user exits) and implicit flavors. Explicit enhancements are spots in standard SAP code which allows for changes. It's very similar to user exits but has the added benefit of being able to be search on as well as collectively grouped in composite enhancements. Moreover, enhancements are part of the standard upgrade process so the system will force the client to at least double check the enhancement post upgrade. There is no such requirement for a user exit or Business Add-In. Implicit enhancements however are NOT clearly defined spots as designated by SAP. They are areas within ANY standard SAP code which can be altered (generally begin or end of coding blocks, events, etc.). The risk is generally higher with implicit enhancements versus explicit enhancements. Reason is that the "context" of what a block of existing code is doing must be taken into consideration while making an implicit enhancement. ANY changes by SAP to that block of code could invalidate / break the enhancement since SAP has no idea what the client may or may not do. So, use with caution.

- If the desire is to enhance a *specific segment* of code does not reveal an explicit enhancement spot nor is it at a generic implicit enhancement location, then the last option would be to physically modify the code (known as "Modification" versus "Enhancement"). Mods are logged in the system and will trigger necessary workload during an upgrade. Mods are generally frowned up in the SAP client base as they are notoriously hard to support. However, based on how the standard SAP code is structured, a modification may be unavoidable to achieve the desired functionality.

Chapter IX – Importance of Change Management

"Whilst technology is a great enabler, it is not a panacea in itself." Stephen Harwood.

What Change Management is

Change management is generally defined as a set of processes that prepare, equip and support individuals to successfully adopt change in order to drive organizational success and outcomes[62]. Good change management practices are critical for a successful SAP Finance implementation.

What Change Management is not

Change does not equal training. Training is a large component of change management but it is not *the sole definition* or solution to effective change management.

Many initiatives at change management in an SAP project tend to be not fully successful for many reasons. One of the reason is to simply assume that change management equals training. Thousands of PowerPoint slides have been created to inform users on how to use a particular set of functionalities without further consideration of *how the materials* on the slides will be learned and applied by users.

Buy-in from Senior Management

To have a successful project it is very important to have senior management buy-in *early on* into the project. Senior management not only from the direct business or corporate line that your SAP finance project will impact, but also buy-in from other groups impacted by this change. Having multiple support from different will ensure a better project and less potential arguments among senior levels of management about this project. Senior management is defined as those reporting to the CEO or two levels below the CEO. Titles usually associated with senior management, include CFO, Controller, EVP of a segment, VP of operations and several others.

Some items to discuss with senior management:

- Have a good project plan laid out plan, with realistic expectations and significant contingencies.

---

[62] https://www.prosci.com/resources/articles/what-is-change-management

- Lay out the risks on the implementation, how they are being mitigated and highlight other risks that cannot be mitigated.
- Factor in an extended warranty period post go-live. Despite a very stringent testing process, many issues will occur during and after go-live for a couple of month-end closes. It is reasonable to expect at least *one year post go-live of stabilization* of the system, particularly if the prior financial application was non-SAP.
- Disclose early in the project that not everything will go to plan and the importance of managing expectations. A new SAP system is not a magic wand that will solve all their problems.
- Start mentally preparing your stakeholders for the worst-case scenario and potentially back up plans. Having that discussion early-on would help as the project progresses and milestones begin to slip.
- Communicate very clearly that for a time, things will seem that they are actually worse than the prior financial system, however, as bugs and users get more comfortable they will see the long-term benefits.
- Get support from senior management for the project and have this support cascaded by their leadership among their direct reports and down the chain of command.

Potential questions to ask senior management:

- What are your expectations from this SAP finance implementation?
- What are the main benefits do you expect to gain from this implementation? Is it efficiency, work effort reduction, compliance & standardization or other?
- What is number 1 thing that this project cannot do wrong, or otherwise, it would be a significant failure?
- How many staff members in your organization do you expect to dedicate to this effort? Will they be fully dedicated or part-time?
- Do you have any other large initiatives running at the same time that could compete for attention or resources as well? Many organizations get an initiative overload and may thing the SAP project is another of the latest management fads, instead of a lasting and impactful change.
- If you had to relative rank functionality from a financial system that you would see as most important, what would those be?
- Are you open and willing to change how previous reports communicated to senior management would look like? What reports

or areas you do not want to change vs. which areas do you want to see change in?

- What has the finance organization struggled in providing in the past? For example, is it headcount reporting, margin reporting, geographical or product reporting? What other areas you would like to see improvement in?

Buy-in from Middle Management

Middle management is also very important in an SAP finance implementation for different factors:

- Middle management usually is the main decider of careers and talent management for most employees. They will decide who gets to support the SAP Finance project from a financial end-customer perspective.

- Middle management usually works *hands-on* with reports that are sent to senior executives, so they are more likely to be in the *depths of the work and data required* to provide those reports to upper management.

- They will likely hear first-hand from direct reports on the progression of the SAP financial project, so having them very well versed on the progress and challenges of the project would be instrumental.

Potential questions to ask middle management:

- When nominating finance representatives to the SAP financial project, what criteria are you using to assign them to this project? Is it systems knowledge, expertise in an area, ability to learn or other?

- What do you see as the biggest challenges with the current financial system?

- How do you expect SAP Finance will help change or improve these challenges?

- What are some of the areas, that if the SAP finance project would not deliver, it would be significantly impactful to that area?

- How prepared are you for change management and for example, not being able to have all the *same information* organized the *same in a report* produced by the new system?

- What are the biggest benefits you are looking to get out of the new SAP finance installation? Is it cost reduction, process improvement, compliance or other?

- What are your thoughts on the company decision for your company to move to SAP? What have you heard from other companies that have implemented SAP?
- If you or your direct reports are using a prior version of SAP, what are the biggest complaints with that SAP system?
- How could this new SAP project address those concerns from that prior system?
- Is your team ready for the substantial changes coming from the current SAP finance project or are they still working on current activities in the current system? It is best to have dedicated staff members from the finance function fully embedded into the SAP Finance project as this should not be a part-time position.
- Do you have good processes in place that structure how data should be created, particularly for master data?

Buy-in from the "trenches"

The "trenches" as commonly referenced, are the day-to-day workers using SAP for variety of different business processes. Throughout the project, it is very important for your project team to create rapport with end-users, since they will likely be testing the system, finding bugs and providing feedback. Creating a strong, amicable working relationship with many of the users would be very important in having a successful project. Many times, in the past, key users "in the trenches" have found some of the most complex bugs and significant errors in prior SAP implementations. These errors or bugs, if caught early enough, can be more easily remediated in a project/development environment than an in a *live productive* environment or even worse if the financial data has been submitted externally.

Potential questions to ask to staff members in the "trenches":

- How do you feel about this SAP Finance implementation?
- After having seen the system or tested the new system, what are your first impressions?
- What is one or several features from the old system that you wish you would have in SAP Finance?
- Do you think the training that has been completed so far has been effective or additional sessions might be needed?

- What would you change in SAP to make it more productive and easier to use?
- What are your colleagues' first impression of SAP so far?
- Any functionality that if not there in SAP would be a complete show stopper?
- What is your biggest challenge in getting things done in SAP?

Criticality of End-User Training

Historically, for many SAP implementations, end-user training has been left towards the very end of the project, leaving very little time for users to get acclimated to the SAP GUI/Fiori or new business processes. End-user training has to be planned out from the beginning, incorporating the ability to translate from the older system to the new SAP Finance system. Long PowerPoints are good for long-term reference and review *after the fact*, but it is critical to deliver *in-person* training for the first set of users so that they can become future potential SME's in SAP.

Staging Training

Many studies have shown that *information overload* is a very common experience. Particularly having staff members sit through multiple days of training on all SAP topics would for sure cause information overload and limit the staff members' ability to retain all that information. It is a better practice to stage the training *throughout* the implementation project. For best information retention it is also advisable to have some sort of hands-on sandbox prototype so that users can get comfortable with Fiori or SAPGUI from the beginning. Most end-user trainings in a project is left towards the very end, but in our opinion that is a mistake. Of course, there will be some developments that are still a work in progress throughout the project, but it is best to have as many frequent trainings throughout a longer period of time than to try to cover everything from logging in to advanced custom SAP programs. With this approach, users will retain more information, be able to practice more along the way and get comfortable with the system. Once users are comfortable with the system and functionality this is one less barrier to gain final user acceptance. The other advantage of staging training throughout the project is that for example, some of the basics on SAP GUI or Fiori could be recorded and have as a reference point for future users of the system.

Delivery methods of Training

In general terms, the most effective training method, particularly when introducing a new concept or development, is to conduct training *in-person* or remotely so that participants can ask questions. For topics that are more generic in place (For example, introduction to the SAP GUI interface, or Fiori interface), it is best to either create CBT's or videos that can be re-used for future users joining the particular controllers' team.

Topics where In-Person/Remote delivery method is preferred (with recorded sessions):

- High complexity customizations, where new concepts are being introduced.

- High degree of complexity in the execution of the steps, where it is not just a matter of executing the program and the program running correctly but understanding the dependencies and final output.

- When the results of execution need to be analyzed and have a lot of context and subject matter expertise in the topic (for example, a program that outputs zero if everything is balanced would not be a good candidate for in-person training)

- Depending on the level of expertise of the audience, the *higher* the discrepancy between the expertise of the presenter and audience, the more suited the concept is for in-person/remote live training.

The following are examples where Computer-Based Training or pre-recorded video training would be best suited:

- Concepts that are more "mechanic" in nature (i.e. click this button, this will do this action, etc.) and thus simpler to replicate.

- Topics at hand that do not require a lot of significant *background knowledge* on a specific process or area. For example, to operate the SAP GUI to a medium level of proficiency does not require to be an SME in a particular financial topic.

- There is a high level of rotation of staff members moving in to new positions that need to acquire base knowledge in the SAP Finance system. This would not be cost effective to have very sought-after SME's cover the same base topics *over* and *over*.

- Audience can work fairly independently if given an initial session. For example, an SME could conduct an initial in-person/remote session of a medium complexity program for new users, and then follow up with links to the pre-recorded trainings for those users to get up to speed.

- The audience is highly knowledgeable in the system already and having a live session would not be the best use of their time.

The high cost of skipping on user training

Reducing end-user training as a way to reduce project costs or time is not sustainable in the long-run. Having a robust and easy to follow training program, that can accommodate users joining at multiple times in the year is quite vital to sustain the return on investment on an SAP finance system.

In prior implementations millions of dollars have gone into designing and implementing highly complex and massive SAP finance systems and left users without proper training. As new users come in and struggle with the system, either data quality goes down over time, features that were built with great care and design go unused or new functionality that already exists in SAP is requested. An SAP system can be thought of as an airplane, highly complex, efficient machine that if used by highly trained staff members will lead to great results. Invest in a great Airbus A380 airplane with poorly trained staff and watch the deterioration and potential safety issues arise over the years.

The high returns of training

From previous projects, training can truly provide a high return on investment on deploying your SAP project. Training is an integral component of change management and enables the proper use an application as complex as S/4 HANA.

The more and more users learn more about the capabilities of SAP, the more knowledgeable they will become and the more thoughtful requests for customizations will be in the future. Training can unleash the power of an ERP system and allow for better designs on future potential developments in the future, which will increase the ROI of a large SAP Finance project.

A couple of examples from the past were training has provided high returns on investment:

- A short 30-minute showcasing a use case for newly developed SAP *S/4 HANA only t-codes* saved analysts more than 5 hours per month in processing time in not having to use Excel.
- A 2-hour course on Analysis for Office, with half of the time with planned material and the remaining time being open Q&A resulted

in 4 analysts learning about a functionality they were not aware. By using this new feature in AO, they were able to save 10 hours per month in their process.

- By being aware of new functionality in S/4 HANA, a customer who was planning on putting a customization request costing $200,000 avoided that expense just by using standard functionality in SAP.

Prototyping and buy-in from end-users

Another area where there is significant buy-in that can be received from end-users is in prototyping. Prototyping can take many ways and phases but could be thought as conducting either configuration or ABAP development efforts in a sandbox or prototype environment. Prototyping allows end-users to see the potential end-result of what a customization might look like and will allow them to refine the eventual requirements.

Follow are general benefits from using prototyping:

- Reduced time and costs: Prototyping improves the quality of the specifications and requirements provided to customers. With prototyping, customers can anticipate higher costs, needed changes and potential project hurdles, and most importantly, potential end result disasters. Strong prototyping can ensure product quality and savings for years to come[63].

- Improved and increased user involvement: Most customer want to feel like they are involved with the intricate details of their project. Prototyping requires user involvement and enables them to see and interact with a working model of their project. With prototypes, customers can give their immediate feedback, request project changes and alter model specifications. Prototyping most importantly helps eliminate misunderstandings and miscommunications during the development process[64].

- Reduced time and costs: Nothing makes customers happier than projects that come in under budget. Prototyping improves the quality of requirements and specifications provided to customers. Needed changes detected later in development cost exponentially

---

[63] From: https://rapidsrepro.com/advantages-disadvantages-prototyping/
[64] IBID

more to implement. With prototyping, you can determine early what the end user wants with faster and less expensive software[65].

Potential ideas for prototyping or demos in SAP:

- Running through an entire transaction from posting the financial entry, to mapping out all the tables and processes that are posted, to running several AO reports based on that entry. This could help users with visualizing how data flows in SAP.

- Have a working session whereby a developer creates a small working program and builds out a selection screen based on customer input. This will improve the user's understanding of how custom programs could be built by the IT team and the importance of thinking about the design early on.

- Designing a quick report with a developer that joins a transactional table with a master data table. For example, joining ACDOCA table with table CSKS/CSKST (cost center table) to obtain cost center information such as cost center description, functional area, tax jurisdiction and much more.

Technical Point of View

Change management from a technical point of view takes on a different bent. It is super critical to be disciplined in this area to avoid negative outcomes. SAP provides a number of standard tools (as well as additional cost tools) to aid in technical change management.

Order Matters

In simplest terms, code changes are captured in "transports" and these transports are moved thru the landscape. One does not make direct changes to production. Changes have to come from the source (development) system. All the systems in the landscape must be kept in sync. And order is most critical when one talks of synchronization. Kindly see the following very basic example.

- Program A was created and captured in transport A.
- Program A was transported to the quality system (in a typical 3 system landscape, the quality assurance system is where testing is done to verify what was done in the development system before moving it into the production system).

---

[65] IBID

- Program B (which happens to call program A) was created and captured in transport B.
- Program B was transported to the quality system for testing. All is well and tested without issue.

Now it is time for go-live. Transport A and B must both be imported IN THAT SEQUENCE. If they were backwards – when transport B is imported – program A would not be there yet and the import will fail since program B has errors due to missing program A. Similarly, both must go. The testing done was based on both programs being in the system and working in tandem. If only transport A was imported into the production system, the import will not fail but the overall solution is lacking because program B is missing. SAP's standard transport management tools in general will keep the sequence correctly. However, the moment the business / stake holders have a say as to what may be imported and what needs to wait – then scenarios as such may arise. If everything released so far are imported, one should generally have little to no issues. If transports are skipped (for whatever reason), then all bets are off. Best case scenario would be an import failure since that would prompt someone to investigate. Worst case scenario would be that the import was successful (just missing some). There is no indication that something is wrong. The user base will use an "incomplete" solution in the productive environment. The outcome is completely unpredictable.

Level of Disruption

Changes sent to a productive landscape can cause disruptions. If the updated object (e.g. program) is being used during the import, the process could cancel with error. This could have a major impact if it was a long running program which the business was waiting on to complete other time sensitive tasks. Another type of disruption would be database changes. Some types of database changes are benign and others can cause the system to halt while the change is being absorbed. Changes as such may need "quiet" time to import (time where no processes are running which may be impacted by the change). Locking users out often is not enough as there are many background processes or interfaces which could also depend on the changed table.

Ageism?

One should never treat someone different based on age. However, this does not apply to changes / transports. The life cycle of change captured in a transport is from beginning (development system) to end (production system). Anytime in between presents risk. It is advised to keep the life span of a change as short as possible. The longer it lingers, the more trouble it could create. Continuing on the earlier example.

- Program A is in the production system
- Program B which calls program A is only in the quality assurance system
- An urgent fix is needed for program A in the production system
- However, changes made to A causes Program B to fail and thus the transport fails during import into the quality assurance system.
- This failure will prevent the much-needed fix to program A from being moved to the production system

Program B has negatively affected the landscape. The longer it sits, the more issues it can create. So, age does matter when it comes to changes and transports.

Chapter X – Performance Testing

"There is often a level of arrogance in ERP consultants who are taken with replacing existing systems, a level of arrogance that is generally counter-productive." Worster, Weirick, Andera.

S/4 Data Model Recap

With the continuous simplification of financial processes and the move of previously separate tables into the universal journal, there are many positive factors from this simplification of the data model:

- Lower data footprint and data storage. By not having to store redundant and duplicative data in other financial tables, S/4 has a reduced data footprint compared to ECC 6.0.
- Simplified custom developments by being able to query from one single table, instead of having to query and/or join multiple tables to arrive at the same results.
- Less data reconciliation between different tables, achieves "single-source of truth" concept.
- Summarization on the "fly" vs. having separate line item records vs. totals.

Performance testing

In a new implementation of SAP S/4 HANA performance testing is a must. Not only is it required since it's an evolving product, by proactively testing and addressing performance issues head-on, your implementation has a higher change of success.

While HANA brings enterprise resource planning software to a different level, it is both the biggest advantage and biggest mission critical component within the SAP landscape.

Prioritization of performance testing

Since not all the programs, either standard SAP or custom, can be fully performance tested from an end-to-end perspective, the following questions can help with which functionality to focus a more time on performance testing:

- What functionality is on the critical path for time-sensitive processes such as month-end close, quarter-end close or year-end close?

- Is a process isolated and does not have any downstream dependencies or stringent deadlines? For example, say some analysis reports have a 1-2-month preparation time, those could potentially have lower priority for performance testing & subsequent optimization.

- What process could not be restarted from where the process was interrupted? As discussed earlier, anything that deals with balances, such as fixed assets, is very difficult to simply "pick-up" from where the process was interrupted. Other processes, such as financial reporting mapping, some settlements, payroll and other processes, can pick up more easily where the last item was processed.

- In what workday of the month-end close is that process expected to be executed? Earlier processes should have a higher focus on performance testing, since any unexpected delays could impact the entire month-end processes and completely delay. The further along in the month-end close, typically, resource intensive processes to plateau in comparison to the earlier processes. For example, if allocations do not run on the expected timeframe, all kinds of issues could arise, up to an unable to report correctly on the financial performance of the different business units or segments of a company.

- What process consumes or produces the highest number of records? Also, are the records being generated to an SAP standard table or a custom table? Processes that write to SAP standard tables should have a higher priority due to the inability of potentially not being able to pick up when interrupted or having bad quality being next to impossible to fix. Those processes that populate records to custom tables can potentially have the contents deleted and started from scratch, which might potentially improve performance. Another concept to keep in mind is that S/4 HANA have incremental performance in terms of *reading data,* but as mentioned earlier, the increment in performance for *writing data* is not as high. Prioritize those processes writing large amounts of data and potentially either reconsider them.

Other considerations

Following are several considerations to take in place for performance testing

- How is your company code structure setup? Do most of the company codes in your implementation are expected to have a highly concentrated number of transactions. For example, if one company code will represent 80% of the volume of transactions in your implementation, if that could potentially be changed that would save several issues down the road. If that company code structure cannot be re-worked, make sure that performance testing always includes that key company code.

- How would test or dummy data be generated to ensure performance testing is representative of real-time conditions? For example, be sure to have in your implementation some sort of custom journal entry upload functionality so that vast number of transactions can be posted to simulate real-life conditions.

Good Days and Bad Days

One big misconception with HANA is that there are no drives involved. The persistence of the data is still on drives. Once powered off, memory holds nothing. So, a HANA appliance is sized in such a way that allows the majority of the needed data to be loaded into memory. Every time the HANA system restarts (whether due to routine maintenance or unforeseen outages), data has to be loaded by to memory so the initial access to data can be slow. Once loaded, the faster / expected query speed returns. Until then, the act of reading data from storage and loading into memory can take time. Moreover, HANA will roll out unneeded data to make room for requested data. So, the adage of every process must play nice comes into play. Large tables can often displace many smaller tables. This brings up the point that there are circumstances (even during regular usage) whereby data must be loaded (due to being displaced or system restart) and thus causes longer runtimes. So, performance testing must be repeated against the same data set to see what the "in memory" speed truly is.

High Horsepower Does Not Excuse Bad Design

Having a technical marvel to make on the fly decisions is great. But that does not mean that HANA is bulletproof. A rogue query or CDS definition can easily consume a large amount of runtime resources and cause overall system slow down. The layered approach to building CDS view hierarchies can also be problematic. When data volume is low (shortly after go-live), the performance could be acceptable. But as volume increases and the runtime lengthens, a rework of the CDS may be difficult because of dependencies caused by these layers. So even if performance of the process in question during testing was good / acceptable, it is no guarantee that it will be that way in the real world.

Every bit counts

One must take the approach within custom development that every single bit of speed is important. Programs should be slim and trim with speed in mind. Not only programs but how data is partitioned also makes a huge difference. Different partitioning schemes are available to avoid the two billion row per table limit HANA currently has. Some schemes are optimized for reading of data while others are optimized for writing. Knowledge of how the data will be accessed and how much should drive this decision.

Proactive Monitoring

Waiting until system comes to a crawl before checking the system health is not ideal. Knowing the performance of the system is directly related to the health of the HANA appliance, it behooves any customer to be proactive about checking the health of various HANA components. Check memory usage, expensive SQL statements, long wait times for processes, etc. These are all simple proactive checks any administrators can do to stay ahead of trouble.

Chapter XI – Summary

"If you think education is expensive, try ignorance." Derek Bok.

The high cost of first entrants

Unlike most other aspects in life, many times, being the first entrant may not fully pay in the long-run. Upgrading an SAP system is a monumental task with lots of complexities and configuration considerations. The other aspect is that SAP is continuously innovating and adding more and more functionality every year or so, so having the first version of a product may not work for very stable corporate customers.

Decision Criteria

There are many aspects to consider *what* to upgrade, *when* to upgrade and *how* to upgrade to a new S/4 HANA system. We hope the discussion over the next couple of pages will help you have better conversations with all the stakeholders involved.

Why Move to S/4 HANA now?

Moving to S/4 HANA now has many advantages, including:

- Reduction in a system's data footprint. Without redundant financial data being replicated in multiple tables, S/4 HANA has a lower storage requirement than ECC 6.0, saving on data storage and replication costs.

- Easier customizations in the finance space. Since the majority of financial/accounting tables have been consolidated into the Universal Journal or ACDOCA table, it makes retrieving, analyzing and creating custom programs easier to do since the majority of financial data is in a single place.

- Learning curve for the organization. Moving to a new system, whether coming from a prior SAP system already or from a non-SAP system is already quite a large endeavor. By moving earlier to S/4 HANA, your company will be able to assess earlier the knowledge gaps about SAP in your IT department as well as your finance customers. If your last large SAP implementation was 20 years ago or longer, you may have an organizational learning gap that needs to be mitigated. If you delay an S/4 HANA implementation, some of the most experienced staff members may have already been retired. By moving earlier, you allow for knowledge continuity and for a new generation of staff members that will support the system to learn on a project, which provides the highest returns in terms of training.

- Ability to influence the roadmap of S/4 HANA. By being a first entrant, you may able to influence future product offerings from SAP.

Are Business processes aligned?

One of the challenges in any IT project, but particularly for ERP implementations is the level of understanding and alignment of various business processes. Business processes are not developed in a "big-bang" approach, instead they develop organically *over many years* and may not be fully understood end-to-end by neither receivers or senders of this financial process. A system implementation can increase in complexity if businesses processes are not aligned, documented or widely understood. For example, since the ultimate goal of a report may not be fully understood, you may be unnecessarily replicating functionality from a prior system that may not be applicable anymore.

The following are potential considerations to factor in for your implementation:

- How many different groups in the Finance or Controllers organization deal with transactional processes?
  - o In general, the more groups that deal with transactional processes, the higher probability of having "different" standards or "this is the way we do it here"
- How often do staff rotate through these groups? The more rotations in and out of these positions, the higher probability of each person adding their flavor. Conversely, the more stable the rotations out of these groups, the higher probability of "stale" business processes (i.e. activities that have been completed just because the predecessor completed them).
- How well documented are your current business processes? Do your customers have a detailed guide or manual? Are business processes consisting of a collection of *emails* and *spreadsheets*? Having bad business processes will not be magically fixed by SAP S/4 HANA.

Moving from a non-SAP system to S/4 HANA

In general, a bigger benefit case, but more challenging project, can be made of moving from a non-SAP system to S/4 HANA. Since HANA is the future of all SAP implementations, it will not make sense to move an earlier version.

Although this migration can provide significantly higher benefits than moving from an existing SAP system, the project complexity increases exponentially.

Just looking at a couple of challenges in this space:

- Higher development costs, since many SAP solutions will have to be created from "scratch" or will have to developed based on the prior system's design.
- Higher change management costs, including not only for end-users but also for your IT team if they themselves are transitioning these systems.
- Much more complex configuration in SAP, having to configure pretty much every FI module that will have to be used. For these types of implementation, these represent a good use case for SAP's model company.
- Higher master data migration efforts, since all new master data will have to be created from zero or roughly based on the prior system.
- Longer project timeframe than a migration from an existing SAP system.
- More complex data conversion, since the financial elements used will have to converted from the prior system to the SAP logic.

Benefits of moving to an S/4 HANA from a non-SAP system:

- Great opportunity to improve business processes and potentially use SAP standard functionality if it meets most critical business needs.
- Potential opportunity, before starting the project, to have robust master data standards, particularly before data conversion and migration is completed.
- Potential to take advantage of analytics tools, such as SAP Analysis for Office, built-in into the ERP, without having to rely on a data warehouse or third-party applications.

Moving from a prior SAP system to S/4 HANA

Although less dramatic than moving from a non-SAP to S/4 HANA system, there are still many benefits of S/4 HANA:

- Reduced data footprint
- Faster retrieve response
- Analytics embedded in the transactional system
- Reduced or eliminated data reconciliations between the former SAP Finance tables and now ACDOCA.
- Ability to quickly sum up millions of lines of data in real time

Technical Point of View

Understand the move to S/4 HANA is not so much a migration but a new setup.   Fundamentally S/4 HANA is different than ECC.   Database architecture is different.   Data model changes. Programming guidelines are tighter. The list goes on. One does not just migrate to S/4 HANA. It generally is a reimplementation or at least have many common elements as a new implementation.

Hardware

S/4 HANA runs on dedicated specialized hardware whereby data is stored in memory (technically on disk but loaded to memory for fast access). Traditional ECC systems can "expand" by adding more disk space. HANA appliances often require new hardware since memory expansion is generally limited based on the vendor/platform. The skillset involved in maintaining this new hardware may be a factor. Operating systems are also different since HANA is only released on various OS versus ECC having a large set of possible OS options.

UNICODE

ECC systems generally recommend UNICODE to be enabled but not required. HANA systems require UNICODE. This in itself can be a project to UNICODE enable all custom development in the ECC system. Moreover, UNICODE takes more space. What was once a 1 TB system will be 2 TB after UC is enabled. Cost again becomes a factor as the size of the HANA appliance needs to accommodate the UC enabled database.

Custom Development

On top of potential UC related changes, the data model change could require custom program changes. Compatibility views are delivered by SAP but often times it is merely a *stop-gap*. There are instances whereby the way SAP operates is different and thus coding will have to change. Moreover, just because a program is syntax error free in a S/4 HANA system does not mean it will perform well.   Pre-HANA days, conventional software design would be to normalize data (i.e. split data up into separate tables for storage). Post HANA days, that's the complete opposite. With data compression, one does not save too much space normalizing data. By having the data split up, it requires now joins to retrieve the necessary data. Whereas HANA based designs would generally have all the data in one place for fastest retrieval possible. The amount of change needed to realize the speed and power of HANA in custom code written for ECC may be high. Consider this in the decision.

Glossary

ACDOCA: The main transactional financial table. Also known as the universal journal. ACDOCA merges prior ECC tables like BKPF, BSEG, COEP, COBK and others, into a single table consisting of more than 400 fields. It forms the basis for reporting of most financial transactions in S/4 HANA. SAP roadmap is to continue transition legacy tables into ACDOCA.

BKPF: Document header table for GL postings. This table is common in both ECC and S/4 HANA systems and holds document header records. As time progresses, this table may in the future get converted to a CDS view for compatibility reasons[66].

BSEG: Document line item table for GL postings. Similar to BKPF, this table is common in both ECC and S/4 HANA. One key aspect to mention is that both BKPF and BSEG form still the main backbone of FI Validations and Substitutions.

Business Area: A business area allows a company to be able to create financial statements and cross company codes. Most generally, the business area is derived from the cost center, but can also be manually input. SAP's roadmap recommends for new SAP customers to not rely too heavily on business area and instead focus on using Segment functionality.

Company Code: A company code can be defined as the *smallest* organizational unit in SAP where a full set of financial statements, that is balance sheet, income statement and cash flow, can be drawn. A company code, traditionally in SAP

Company Code Branch: A company code created for any other purpose (internal reporting for example) than to represent a legal entity. Company code branches are a very powerful concept used by many SAP customers since it is the surest way to be able to generate a fully balanced set of financial statements (balance sheet and income statement). It remains to be seen whether with document splitting in the future, potentially customers may not need branches but could rely on other SAP elements.

---

[66] As of the time of this writing both BKPF and BSEG are still traditional tables and have not transitioned to CDS views like other tables.

CO Module: SAP module used for cost management accounting & reporting. Cost center, profit center and internal order accounting takes place in the CO Module.

Cost Center: A cost center represents a location where the costs are incurred inside an organization. Cost centers can represent responsibility areas and are used to capture actual costs as they are posted.

COEP: table that holds CO document line items. In S/4 COEP table is merged into table ACDOCA.

COBK: a table that holds CO document headers. Similar to COEP, this table is now merged into ACDOCA.

Data Conversion: process whereby data from the prior system is converted to the new system. Data is converted, created and posted into the new system.

Document Splitting: SAP technology, that initially came with new GL in the mid 2000's. Document splitting allows an FI document to be "fully balanced" beyond the company code, using elements such as profit center, business area and many others.

ERP: Enterprise Resource Planning. Basically a collection of applications that centralizes businesses process into a single system.

General Ledger: A general ledger holds a record of all the financial transactions posted for a particular time period. From a general ledger a trial balance and financial statements can be generated from.

Profit Center: a profit center allows a customer to determine the profit and loss for different responsibility areas within an organization. A profit center, unlike a cost center, can cross company codes.

Project Systems (PS) module: module within SAP used to create projects, prepare budgets and record actuals.

Internal Order: internal orders are temporary cost objects that can be used to collect costs and revenues for specific circumstances within an organization. For example, an internal order can be setup to track specific type of costs to increase their visibility and allow for planning.

General Accounting: Typically an accounting function that deals with recording accounting transactions in areas such as fixed assets, intercompany reconciliation, account reconciliations and financial statement consolidation and creation.

NetWeaver: NetWeaver is the technical foundation for many of SAP products, including SAP ERP and S/4 HANA. NetWeaver is the runtime environment for solutions such as S/4 HANA, ERP, ECC and several other SAP products.

ECC 6.0: Initially released in 2006, it is the most widely spread ERP system used in the world by many industries and businesses[67].

OSS Notes: Stands for Online Service System, which provide SAP users with Knowledge Base Articles (KBA), an incident portal to create and monitor incidents or bugs reported to SAP as well software downloads.

R/2: A prior version of SAP ERP software released in the early 1980's. It was replaced by R/3 in the early 1990's[68].

R/3: SAP's ERP version released in the 1990's with significant improvements over R/2, including the ability to run on servers instead of mainframes and the concept of quasi-real time update of totals and line items.

S/4 HANA: Successor release of SAP R/3 ECC 6.0 and SAP ERP, organized to take advantage of SAP's in-memory database HANA. In S/4, several modules, including Financials, are streamlined from a data model perspective to reduce data redundancy and take advantage of HANA new capabilities.

Segment: Reporting unit in SAP Finance, associated with a profit center, that allows a company to produce business segment financial statements, with a fully balanced balance sheet and income statement. Segment, along with profit center, business area and other elements, is one of the dimensions that can be configured for document splitting balancing.

Single Source of Truth: Reference to the universal journal or ACDOCA table. Labeled this way since there is no need for data reconciliation for several key processes as it used to be in prior versions of SAP ECC 6.0

Suite on HANA: Functionality whereby an existing ECC 6.0 system's database is replaced from a traditional disk-based storage is replaced with HANA's in memory database, thereby improving the speed of the existing

---

[67] https://sapservices.scalefocus.com/sap-ecc/
[68] https://www.sap.com/about/company/history/1981-1990.html

SAP installation. Suite on HANA are also implemented for Business Warehouse solutions, being that the existing BW cubes can achieve significant performance improvement by switching from a disk-based database to an in-memory database like HANA.

Universal Journal: Also known as ACDOCA. See ACDOCA definition.

Index